Summer Bridge Reading
Grades 5–6

Editor: Julie Kirsch

Layout Design: Tiara Reynolds

Inside Illustrations: Magen Mitchell

Cover Design: Chasity Rice

Cover Illustration: Wayne Miller

ISBN 978-1-60022-448-5

Table of Contents

The *Summer Bridge Reading* series is designed to help children improve their reading skills during the summer months and between grades. *Summer Bridge Reading* includes several extra components to help make your child's study of reading easier and more inviting.

For example, an **Assessment** test has been included to help you determine your child's reading knowledge and what skills need improvement. Use this test, as well as the **Assessment Analysis**, as a diagnostic tool for those areas in which your child may need extra practice.

Furthermore, the **Incentive Contract** will motivate your child to complete the work in *Summer Bridge Reading*. Together, you and your child choose the reward for completing specific sections of the book. Check off the pages that your child has completed, and he or she will have a record of his or her accomplishment.

Examples are included for each new skill that your child will learn. The examples are located in blue boxes at the top of the pages. On each page, the directions refer to the example your child needs to complete a specific type of activity.

Summer Reading List

Aiken, Joan
The Wolves of Willoughby
Chase

Armstrong, Jennifer
Shipwreck at the Bottom of
the World: The Extraordinary
True Story of Shackleton and
the Endurance

Babbitt, Natalie
Tuck Everlasting

Brashares, Ann
The Sisterhood of the
Traveling Pants series

Cabot, Meg
The Princess Diaries series

Craven, Margaret
I Heard the Owl Call My
Name

Cushman, Karen
Catherine, Called Birdy

Dahl, Roald
Matilda

Durbin, William
The Broken Blade

Fleischman, John
Phineas Gage: A Gruesome
but True Story about Brain
Science

Greene, Bette
Summer of My German
Soldier

Henkes, Kevin
Words of Stone

Hesse, Karen
Stowaway

Hinton, S. E.
The Outsiders

Jensen, Dorothea
The Riddle of Penncroft Farm

Juster, Norton
The Phantom Tollbooth

Korman, Gordon
I Want to Go Home!;
The Twinkie Squad

Lindgren, Astrid
Pippi Longstocking

London, Jack
The Call of the Wild

Lowry, Lois
The Giver;
Number the Stars

McKinley, Robin
The Blue Sword

Montgomery, L. M.
Anne of Green Gables

O'Dell, Scott
The Black Pearl

Paterson, Katherine
Bridge to Terabithia

Paulsen, Gary
Hatchet;
The Island

Pullman, Philip
The Golden Compass

Rawls, Wilson
Where the Red Fern Grows

Rubin, Robert Alden
Poetry Out Loud

Sleator, William
House of Stairs

Snyder, Zilpha Keatley
The Egypt Game;
The Velvet Room

Speare, Elizabeth George
The Witch of Blackbird Pond

Spinelli, Jerry
Maniac Magee;
Wringer

Stanley, Diane
Michelangelo

Taylor, Mildred D.
Roll of Thunder, Hear My Cry

Tolkien, J. R. R.
The Hobbit

Travers, P. L.
Mary Poppins

Whelan, Gloria
Listening for Lions

White, Ruth
Belle Prater's Boy

Zindel, Paul
The Pigman and Me

Assessment Test

Read the following passage and answer questions 1–10.

We are destroying our personal link to the future. How can that be? It is disintegrating because we do not write. Think for a moment about how we know about the personal lives of the people who lived before our time. We know what these people did, ate, saw, wore, and believed, because they wrote about it. Throughout history, people have left records of their lives. Some wrote letters to loved ones who lived far away. Pioneers kept diaries and journals that depicted their treacherous, sometimes deadly journey as they trudged across the United States in search of better lives. Soldiers wrote letters home describing the horrors of war. The words of our ancestors have survived the years, and as we read their accounts, we see a glimpse of what their lives were like.

Today, with the advent of new technology, writing has become less common. Instead, many people communicate via phone, e-mail, or text message. Our words disappear as soon as they are spoken or deleted. If we want future generations to know about the lives we've lived, we need to leave a written legacy. It's up to each of you. Pick up a pen and write a letter to a friend or family member. Start a diary or a journal and record what you do each day. These events may seem trivial to you, but they might hold great insight for your descendents. Imagine your great-great-great-grandchild reading your journal more than 100 years from now and enjoying what you wrote. Start today. Write. Create your own personal link to the future.

1. What is the main idea? _people today should write more lives._

2. Underline the topic sentence. _to provided link for future generations._

3. List three details that support the main idea. _people made diaries, wrote letters about there life, and people made text messa_

4. Look up the word *link* in a dictionary. Write two meanings for this word.

   _____

   _____

5. Underline the part of the following sentence that is the cause. Draw a box around the part of the sentence that is the effect.

   We will not have a personal link to the future if we do not write.

6. What is the author's purpose? _____

Assessment Test (continued)

7. *Down-to-earth* is an idiom that describes a type of person. What do you think it means?

_____

_____

8. Summarize the article. _____

_____

_____

_____

_____

_____

_____

9. Compare and contrast something else that we do differently from our ancestors. Draw and fill in a Venn diagram to depict the similarities and differences.

10. On another sheet of paper, write at least two paragraphs that explain your Venn diagram. Be sure the paragraph includes a main idea and supporting details.

© Rainbow Bridge Publishing   Summer Bridge Reading RB-904096

Assessment Test (continued)

Read the following passage and answer questions 11–15

"Let's see . . . 25, 50, 75, 80, 81, 82 . . . . That's $47.82," counted Cal. He gathered the change and placed it next to the bills on the red comforter. Then, he flopped back onto the bed, making the change bounce.

"Rats! We still need $12.18 to cover the admission cost," pouted Leo. "Mom said that we have to have the total cost of admission before we can go to the Greatest Theme Park Ever." The two lay on the floor in Cal's room, imagining the theme park: great junk food like chili dogs, cotton candy, frozen drinks, and elephant ears; games that offer prizes of oversized stuffed animals; and the rides, oh, the rides—wild roller coasters, spinning swings, and Ferris wheels!

"We won't have enough money with our allowances for two more weeks," said Cal. "Besides, that doesn't leave anything for food or souvenirs."

"I know," Leo said, "and I've already checked between the couch cushions, under the car seats, and in all of our jacket pockets." The two sat in mutual gloom. They watched the colorful leaves drop outside the window. Suddenly, they had an idea.

11. Which of the following events happens next to last?

   A. The boys have an idea.

   B. The boys watch the leaves drop outside.

   C. The boys count their money.

12. List three things the boys would like do at the amusement park. _____

   _____

   _____

13. What is the setting of the story? _____

14. What idea do you think the boys have at the end of the story? _____

   _____

15. Do you think that the boys are brothers? _____

   Circle the detail in the story that supports your answer.

Summer Bridge Reading RB-904096   © Rainbow Bridge Publishing

Assessment Review

Check Assessment Test answers using the answer key. Match the questions with incorrect answers to the sections. To provide extra practice in problem areas, refer to the pages listed under each section.

1. People today should write more to provide a link for future generations of people.
2. The following sentence should be underlined: *We are destroying our personal link to the future.*
3. Answers will vary, but may include: Throughout history, people have left written records of their lives. Some people wrote letters to loved ones far away. Pioneers kept diaries and journals. Soldiers wrote about the horrors of war. Writing has become less common with the advent of new technology.
4. A relationship between people, events, or situations that connects them in some way; A ring or piece of a chain
5. cause—if we do not write; effect—we will not have a personal link to the future.
6. to persuade readers to write
7. Answers will vary, but should include the idea that someone who is down-to-earth is not pretentious or arrogant.
8.–10. Answers will vary.
11. B.
12. The boys would eat junk food, play games, and ride amusement-park rides.
13. The boys' home
14. The boys will rake leaves to earn the extra money that they need.
15. yes; they have the same mother.

Number(s)	Skill	Activity Page(s)
1–3, 10	main idea and supporting details	51–55
4	multiple-meaning words	17–18
5	cause and effect	31–32
6	author's viewpoint and word choice	69
7	understanding idioms	35–36
8	summarizing	70–74
9	interpreting a Venn diagram	87–88
11	sequencing	19–24
12, 15	reading for details	21–24, 42–50, 56–58
13	story elements	38–41
14, 15	making inferences and predicting outcomes	61–67

Summer Bridge Reading RB-904096

Incentive Contract

List your agreed-upon incentive for each section below. Place an X after each completed exercise.

	Activity Title	X	My Incentive Is:
9	What Was the Question?		
10	Healthy Cookbook		
11	Do What?		
12	What You Read		
13	Plant Life Cycle		
17	Looking It Up		
18	Play Ball		
19	Applesauce		
20	Doggone Tired		
21	Find a Penny		
23	Roller Coasters		
25	Reporting Out		
26	Is That a Fact?		
27	Microscopic		
28	Stretching It?		

	Activity Title	X	My Incentive Is:
51	Rocks in the Head		
52	Infectious Disease		
53	Turn Up the Power		
54	Vertebrates		
56	Asthma		
59	Great Lakes		
61	Housefly		
62	What Is It?		
63	Waiting		
64	Matter		
66	Ladybug Letter		
68	Three Levels of Questions		
69	Camping on Frog Pond		
70	Check Your Summary		
71	Summary Focus		

	Activity Title	X	My Incentive Is:
29	Kick the Can		
31	One after Another		
32	Friendly Conversation		
33	Unfamiliar Words		
34	Wise Words		
35	Figures of Speech		
36	Idioms		
37	Awesome Analogies		
38	Milkweed		
39	Getting the Setting		
40	Within Time		
41	What's the Problem?		
42	My New Companion		
44	Go, Bones!		
46	Babe Didrikson Zaharias		
48	Water around Us		

	Activity Title	X	My Incentive Is:
72	Eyes on You		
73	Bamboo		
75	Sunset		
76	Mountain Reminiscence		
78	Poetry Terms		
80	Winter Sunrise		
81	Guide Words		
82	Library Work		
83	Navigating the Library's Research Section		
84	Parts of a Book		
85	Touch Points		
87	Opinion Papers		
89	African American Time Line		
91	Bicycle Safety		
92	Sleep Tight		

Summer Bridge Reading RB-904096

What Was the Question?

Read each question and identify what is being asked. Underline the key word in the question. Circle the letter next to the best answer.

1. On what date did the travelers land on Saturn?
   A. the Orbiter   B. June 27, 2067   C. from Earth

2. In which city do the Red Sox play?
   A. Fenway Park   B. Massachusetts   C. Boston

3. What company would you call to order new gloves?
   A. 1-800-555-2191   B. Glove Works   C. Chicago, Illinois

4. At what temperature should you bake the cookies?
   A. 350°F   B. 10 minutes   C. in the oven

5. When does the doughnut shop close?
   A. 45th Street   B. Doughnuts Unlimited   C. 6:00 P.M.

6. How long must the research paper be?
   A. Friday at 2:30 P.M. B. two pages   C. typed

7. Where should you sign your name on a check?
   A. on the bottom right line   B. in cursive   C. with a pen

8. Which direction should you turn on Taft Street to go to the museum?
   A. east   B. three blocks   C. over the bridge

9. What color should your rear bicycle reflector be?
   A. circular   B. to the left of the wheel   C. red

10. What is the cost of a local toll call?
    A. 555-1234   B. listen for the dial tone   C. 35¢

11. What is on the menu for lunch?
    A. at noon   B. spaghetti   C. $1.75

12. Which ocean borders North America?
    A. Pacific   B. Western Hemisphere   C. South America

Summer Bridge Reading RB-904096

Use the table of contents to answer the following questions.

1. On what page does the section "Breads and Rolls" begin? _28_

2. On what page does the "Desserts" section end? _126_

3. Which section begins on page 151? _Just for Kids_

4. How many pages are in the section "Vegetables"? _253_

5. The recipe for blueberry muffins is not under "Appetizers" or "Desserts." In which other section could it be? _Cakes and Pies_

6. Which section would you check for a play clay recipe? _____

7. Cherry torte was not in the "Cakes and Pies" section. Where else could it be? _____

8. You have the book open to page 67. Which section are you in? _____

9. Name a recipe you might find on page 70. _____

10. Name a recipe you might find on page 240. _____

11. Name a recipe you might find on page 101. _____

12. What is the quickest way to find a specific recipe? _____

Table of Contents

Do What?

Read and follow each set of directions below.

1. Circle the words whose second letters come alphabetically before the first.
   milk   tea   water   soda   juice

2. Draw a box around the misspelled word.
   ancient   vowle   similar   phonics   alphabetical

3. Underline the words that are similar in meaning to "undivided."
   undone   complete   partial   entire   unfinished

4. Draw an X on each word that does not rhyme with "though."
   through   blew   grow   tough   enough

5. Draw a triangle to the right of the word that is not a continent.
   Antarctica   Europe   Asia   China   Africa

6. Draw a quadrilateral around the word that is not a vertebrate.
   tarantula   koala   manatee   salamander   penguin

7. Draw a star above the word that is not a planet.
   Venus   Mercury   Orion   Uranus   Neptune

8. Draw one line horizontally through each item that is not found in a dictionary.
   definition   biography   diorama   diagram   pronunciation

9. Draw an S on each word that describes matter in the solid state.
   wood   ice   milk   paper   oxygen

10. Draw a flower around the word that is not part of a plant.
    seed   root   leaf   stem   pedal

What You Read

> The **Stroop Effect** says that once you can read, your brain pays more attention to the written word than to its context. Perform a simple experiment to see if this is true.

Follow the directions below. Write the words on a separate sheet of paper in one or two columns.

1. Write the word *blue* with a red crayon.

2. Write the word *white* with a black crayon.

3. Write the word *gray* with a yellow crayon.

4. Write the word *green* with a blue crayon.

5. Write the word *yellow* with an orange crayon.

6. Write the word *pink* with a green crayon.

7. Write the word *red* with a black crayon.

8. Write the word *brown* with an orange crayon.

9. Write the word *tan* with a purple crayon.

10. Write the word *orange* with a green crayon.

11. Write the word *purple* with a blue crayon.

12. Write the word *black* with a red crayon.

Ask five people to look at your list and tell you the color in which each word is written as quickly as they can. According to the Stroop Effect, most people will say the word that is written rather than the name of the color that the word is written in. For example, when looking at the first word, most people will probably say "blue" instead of "red."

Fill in the table to show what you found.

Name	Number Correct	Number Incorrect

Plant Life Cycle

All living things have a cycle of life. Each step allows the next. The life cycle is continuous, with enough members of the species surviving each step to allow the species to survive. Read the description of the plant life cycle. Use the information to complete the activities (pages 15–16).

Plants are found worldwide in many climates and locations, from forests to deserts to mountaintops to swamps. The list of locations and types of plants is seemingly endless, but all of these plants have a common factor: they start their lives as seeds.

The seed provides a safe haven for the defenseless baby plant. Each seed has three main parts: a seed coat, a cotyledon, and an embryo. The seed coat is the outer layer of the seed. It protects the seed from rough or extreme weather and from animal digestive tracts. The cotyledon, or stored food, takes up most of the space inside the seed. It will provide the germinating seed with the energy that it needs to push through soil or other plant matter. The cotyledon also provides the seed with the nourishment that it needs to begin to grow. The third part of the seed is the embryo. The embryo is the baby plant. It has an embryo root that will eventually push its way out of the seed coat, an embryo stem, and embryo leaves, which will later start food production.

The seed will germinate, or begin to grow, when the time is right. It requires three things to germinate: water, warmth, and a good location. Water is needed to soften the seed coat so that the embryo root can poke out of the seed and begin its descent into the soil. New roots grow quickly, which helps them absorb even more water. As the embryo plant grows, the softened seed coat splits open. The seed must also be in a good location with rich soil and a climate that is the right temperature. Warm temperatures are needed to sustain the young plant as it grows. Temperatures that are too cold will end the life cycle by killing the plant.

After the young plant breaks through the soil, it is called a seedling. The seedling has three main parts: roots, a stem, and seed leaves. The seed leaves are often different in shape from the other leaves that will later grow on the plant. The new seedling needs three things to survive. First, it needs the correct amount of water; too much water causes drowning, and too little water causes the seedling to dry up. Second, the seedling needs warm temperatures which will allow the seedling to grow. Third, it needs food. The seedling begins with the stored food from the seed and will eventually make its own food as it grows into a larger plant.

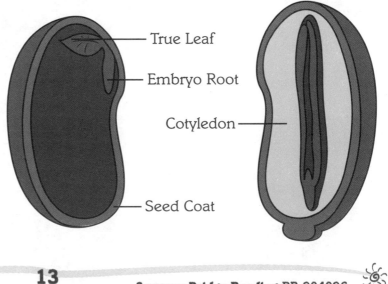

True Leaf

Embryo Root

Cotyledon

Seed Coat

As the seedling grows into a plant, many changes take place. The plant parts begin to perform their own specialized jobs. The roots grow down into the soil and hold the plant in the ground. They are the stabilizing force against wind, weather, and grazing animals. The roots also assist the plant by absorbing water and minerals from the soil. The leaves begin their job—they make and store food. Leaves use the water and minerals absorbed by the roots, carbon dioxide in the air, and sunlight to make food in their chlorophyll. This process uses the carbon dioxide produced by animals, automobiles, and factories to make the oxygen needed by animals. The stem holds up the plant and becomes the distribution center, carrying water and minerals from the roots and produced food from the leaves to the parts of the plant that need them.

Seeds are produced by specialized parts of adult plants. Seeds can be produced in cones or flowers. Cones are produced by evergreen plants. After they have been pollinated by wind, insects, or animals, flowers develop pods, fruits, or vegetables, which house the new seeds. The seeds are then scattered to a new location where the cycle can continue. They can be scattered by animals, birds, wind, water, people, or gravity. Some seeds are eaten by animals or birds and pass through their digestive tracts in their waste. Other seeds, like burs, hitch a ride on fur, feathers, or socks. People also intentionally scatter seeds in gardens. The wind blows other seeds that are specially adapted to travel like small parachutes or umbrellas. Others float on freshwater streams or ocean currents to new locations. Spherical seeds use gravity to drop and roll. Each method of movement ensures enough space for the new generation to grow without crowding the older plants.

Then, when the time is right, a seed will begin to germinate, a seedling will grow, and the cycle will continue.

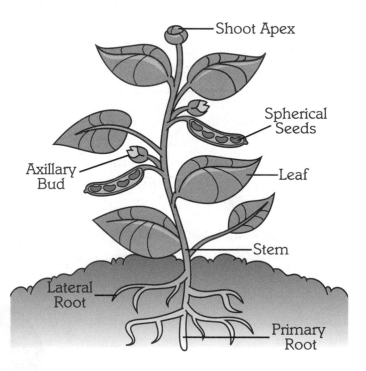

Answer the following questions using information from the article (pages 13–14). Verify your answers by highlighting in the text where you found the information.

1. Where do seed plants grow? List six places. You may use two from the article.

_____   _____

_____   _____

_____   _____

Circle the letter next to the answer.

2. Roots have two main jobs. They
    A. absorb water and make food.
    B. absorb water and hold the plant in the ground.
    C. make and store food in the ground.

3. Where do seeds form?
    A. flowers and cones
    B. stems and roots
    C. leaves and the cotyledon

4. Leaves have two main jobs. They
    A. make and store food.
    B. carry food and water.
    C. absorb water and food.

5. Stems have three main jobs. They
    A. hold up plant parts, absorb water, and carry water.
    B. hold up plant parts, carry water, and carry food.
    C. absorb water, carry water, and carry food.

6. How does water get into the plant?
    A. The roots absorb water that travels through tubes to the rest of the plant.
    B. The roots, stem, and leaves all absorb water for their own uses.
    C. The leaves make and store water.

Plant Life Cycle

Follow the directions to create a poster of the plant life cycle. Check off each step as you complete it.

_____ Write "Plant Life Cycle" in the center of the paper.

_____ Write your first and last names in the bottom right corner.

_____ Divide the paper into six sections. Label them in this order: seed parts, seed germination, seedling, seed plant, seed production, and seed scattering.

Continue to follow the directions by completing each of the following steps in the appropriate section.

_____ Draw a seed. Show and label the three parts of the seed.

_____ Draw a germinating seed.

_____ Write the three things that a seed needs in order to germinate.

_____ Draw and label a seedling. Include roots, stem, and seed leaves.

_____ List the three things a seedling needs in order to grow.

_____ Draw and label a plant. Include leaves, stem, and roots.

_____ Label the two jobs of a leaf.

_____ Include the three things that a leaf needs in order to make food.

_____ Label the two jobs of the root system.

_____ Label the two jobs of a stem.

_____ Draw and label the two plant parts that produce seeds.

_____ List the three things that a flower can make to house its seeds.

_____ List six ways that seeds are scattered.

_____ Draw a representation of one way that seeds are scattered.

_____ Draw an arrow from each section to the next one that happens.

Looking It Up

> Words often have more than one dictionary meaning. The **context** of a passage determines a word's meaning.

Circle the best meaning for each boldfaced word.

1. The **last** tooth that Will lost was an eyetooth. Now, a bicuspid is loose.

   A. the final one

   B. the previous one

   C. the one that endures

2. The hamster looked cold. Selena decided to **line** its box with cotton.

   A. to cover the inner surface

   B. a short letter

   C. the straight two-dimensional figure between two points

3. The smell of freshly **ground** coffee was wafting through the house. "It smells good," thought Jamal. "It's too bad it tastes so awful."

   A. a basis for a belief

   B. the surface of the earth

   C. smashed into small bits

4. Ainslee was studying a honeycomb **cell**. It was incredible to look at it with a magnifying glass.

   A. a small protoplasmic portion of a living organism

   B. a small compartment

   C. the smallest unit of an organization

5. The movie was **over**. It was time to go to bed.

   A. finished

   B. in a position above

   C. to move from a vertical to a horizontal position

6. The test was nearly over. Kyle was trying to **rack** his brain for an answer to the second question. He just could not come up with one.

   A. to think under emotional stress

   B. to fly in high wind

   C. a framework on which things are placed

17

Play Ball

> Even small words can lead to confusion when they have more than one meaning.

Read the paragraph. Use the context to determine the meanings of the bold words. Circle the letter next to each correct definition.

Mia was getting ready to **bat**. She **planted** her feet in the **box** and got ready to **swing**. Kim threw a **strike** across home **plate**. The next two pitches were **balls**. Mia connected with the last **pitch** and ran to first **base**. She hit in the winning **run**.

1. bat
   A. a flying mammal
   B. to take a turn at bat
   C. a stick used to hit a ball

2. planted
   A. dug a hole and placed a seed in the ground
   B. a factory or workshop
   C. fixed in place

3. box
   A. a cardboard rectangular prism
   B. an area next to home plate
   C. to punch another person

4. swing
   A. to move a stick toward a ball
   B. a type of music
   C. a seat attached to two chains

5. strike
   A. a pitch that crosses the plate within a certain range
   B. to hit forcefully
   C. to delete something

6. plate
   A. to coat with metal
   B. a circular object that holds food
   C. a square on the ground used to mark a base

7. balls
   A. pitches thrown that do not pass within a certain range
   B. spherical objects
   C. large, formal gatherings

8. pitch
   A. a musical tone
   B. a ball thrown to a batter
   C. to fall headlong

9. base
   A. the bottom part of an object
   B. one of the four stations on a ball field
   C. lowly or vile

10. run
    A. to move legs rapidly
    B. to move in a melted state
    C. a score made after reaching home plate

Applesauce Recipe

Ingredients:

- 10–17 tart, firm cooking apples (Macintosh, Spy, Jonathan, or Granny Smith)

- 2 cups sugar

- 1 teaspoon cinnamon (more or less to taste)

- 1 cup liquid (water, apple juice, or apple cider)

Also needed: a paring knife, a large soup kettle with a cover, a colander, a wooden mallet, a spatula, a large mixing bowl, a spoon or scoop, measuring tools, and jars or plastic containers for storage

Directions:

Rinse apples and cut into quarters. Do not peel. Remove cores. Fill the large soup kettle with the apples. Add sugar, cinnamon, and liquid. Cover and simmer on medium heat until apples are no longer firm. Stir frequently. Add more liquid if the mixture becomes too thick. Remove from heat. Set colander in a large bowl. Fill the colander half full with apple mixture. Roll the wooden mallet through the apple mixture, pressing out the applesauce. Roll firmly until peelings are dry. Remove peelings from mallet and colander before adding more cooked apples. Continue until apple mixture has been mashed. Scoop applesauce into jars or plastic containers. Refrigerate for up to one week or freeze for several months.

Highlight one key word or phrase for each direction in the text. Then, number the directions below to put them in the correct sequence.

____ Fill the colander with cooked apples.

____ Simmer the apples until they are mushy.

____ Cut the apples into quarters.

____ Refrigerate the applesauce.

____ Add sugar, cinnamon, and liquid.

____ Use water to clean the apples.

____ Place the apples in a pot.

Summer Bridge Reading RB-904096

Doggone Tired

Read the passage.

Kelly and Taffy are dogs. Kelly is a purebred Pembroke Welsh corgi, and Taffy is half dachshund and half beagle. Kelly likes to roll around on the ground, and Taffy likes to run. Taffy especially likes it when Kelly chases her. Their favorite place is the backyard. From the top of a hill in the middle of the backyard, they can see almost the entire neighborhood. Taffy sits on the hill for hours and watches the birds soar, the squirrels hop between trees, and children play. When other dogs walk by, Kelly and Taffy stand together on the hill and bark until the other dogs disappear down the street.

One day, Kelly dug a tunnel under the backyard fence. Taffy saw Kelly go under the fence and followed her out of the backyard. They ran as fast as they could down the street, chasing each other and barking. They saw the mail carrier and barked at him as they ran past. Taffy saw a squirrel and chased it up a tall oak tree. Kelly followed, but she was tired of running and sat down under the tree. Taffy was panting from all of the running and barking, so she sat down, too. They sat back-to-back so that they could face opposite directions. As far as they could see, there was no water and no food. They were very thirsty.

Kelly started walking back, trying to find the hole in the fence. Taffy followed. They looked at many fences, but none had a hole under it.

None of the yards smelled like home either. Thirsty and tired, they sat down under a tree beside the road. The mail carrier drove past and saw them. He stopped his truck and walked over to them. They just looked up at him without barking.

"Ah ha," he said. "Got yourselves lost, did you?" He picked them up and took them home in the mail truck. He led them to the yard and put a big rock in the hole under the fence. Kelly and Taffy ran straight to their water bowl. As the mail carrier drove off, he saw them sitting on top of the hill in the middle of the yard again.

Number the events listed below to put them in the correct sequence.

_____ Kelly and Taffy ride on the mail truck.

_____ The dogs become thirsty and tired.

_____ The mail truck drives off, and the mail carrier sees the dogs sitting on top of the hill again.

_____ Kelly digs a tunnel under the backyard fence.

_____ Taffy chases a squirrel up an oak tree.

_____ The mail carrier speaks to the dogs.

_____ The mail carrier puts a big rock in the hole under the fence.

_____ Taffy follows Kelly out of the backyard.

Find a Penny

Read the passage.

Ben was walking to school with some friends. They saw a bright, shiny penny on the sidewalk. Ben stepped on it.

"Hey," said Mia. "Aren't you going to pick it up?"

"Right," said Ben sarcastically. "'Find a penny; pick it up. Then, all day long you'll have good luck.' If it were a quarter, maybe . . ." He kicked the penny toward the sewer grate and they continued on their way.

They heard the first bell as they rounded the corner to the school. They started running. On the way up the steps, Ben tripped and fell, and his backpack went flying. He limped down the hallway after Amber, Trey, and Paige. The last bell rang as Ben hit the door. "Tardy, Ben," said Ms. Davis. "One more and you will have an extra assignment." The classroom phone rang. As Ms. Davis turned her back to the doorway to answer it, Erin quietly slipped into the classroom and took her seat. She wiped her brow and gave a thumbs-up to Amber. She had narrowly escaped an extra assignment. "Let's begin by handing in our reading assignments," Ms. Davis said as she turned back toward them. Ben pulled out his folder. His assignment was nowhere to be found! "But I spent three hours working on it last night," he wailed.

The morning went from bad to worse. During a three-minute fact test, Ben's pencil lead fell out. Returning from the sharpener, he saw Erin put down her pencil and turn over her test. He wrote two answers, and time was called. During science, his tray tipped over. Dirt, water, a plant, and science tools fell to the floor. An intercom announcement preceded the lunch bell. "The following students' artwork has been selected for the City Art Fair: Haley Goodbrush, Gil Claymore, Erin Coinfinder. . . ."

Erin requested a piece of pepperoni pizza. "Wow, huge slice!" she said. "Yum! Looks good," thought Ben. He asked for one, too. "Sorry," said Mr. Bentley, "I just served the last one."

Ben flopped into a seat next to his friends. He eyed Erin's cheese-laden entrée. "You sure seem to be having a good day today," he muttered.

Erin laughed, "Yeah, you'll never guess what I picked up next to a sewer grate this morning."

Find a Penny

Answer the following questions about the story (page 21).

1. What kind of day is Ben having?_____

Highlight with blue specific details in the story that support your answer.

2. What event foreshadows Ben's day? _____

3. What kind of day is Erin having?_____

Highlight with yellow three details in the story that support your answer.

4. What does Erin pick up? _____

5. What do you think Ben will do the next time he sees a penny? _____

_____

Explain your answer.

_____

_____

_____

Number the events below to put them in the correct sequence.

_____ Ben misses out on pepperoni pizza.

_____ Ben's science tray tips over.

_____ Erin comes into class late.

_____ Ben trips on the school steps.

_____ An announcement is made that Erin's artwork will be in the City Art Fair.

_____ Ben kicks a penny.

_____ Erin completes her math facts quiz.

_____ Ben cannot find his reading assignment.

Roller Coasters

Read the passage.

You are strapped in a seat. A padded bar comes down over your shoulders, allowing minimal movement. Your shoulder itches, but you can't reach it. There is a sudden jerk, and you begin to move forward slowly. Your body tilts until you are looking straight up into a bank of clouds. Your body tenses. Anticipation causes your stomach to roll as you hear a steady *click, click, click* and slowly climb higher and higher. You reach the top, and the pause seems to last forever. You are catapulted forward, dropping down at a speed that causes your stomach to sink. The passing wind slicks back your hair and brings tears to your eyes. The pressure stretches the skin on your face toward the back of your scalp. After a lifetime of seconds, you are at the bottom, racing forward into a series of loops that won't allow your thinking brain to catch up to your emotional body. It's over. It was 120 seconds of adrenaline that seemed to last forever. You climb out of the seat on shaky legs. A relieved body and mind finally find each other. Should you go again? Of course, you go back to wait in the two-hour line.

Roller coasters are quick trips into total feeling and fear. More than 300 million people ride them each year to please peers or family members, to prove courage, or just for fun. Monster coasters tower over amusement parks worldwide.

Roller coasters originated in Russia. This country of many weather extremes found ice sledding to be a popular sport. In the 1400s, hills were built from wooden frames and covered with hard-packed snow. Water was sprayed onto the snow to create a frozen, downward pathway of increasing speed. Some hills reached 70 feet high and were as steep as today's roller coasters. After a climb to the top, the customer rode down on a two-foot-long sled while sitting on a guide's lap. Accidents did happen, but the sport continued. In the 1700s, colorful lanterns allowed for night sledding in busy Saint Petersburg. People could not get enough of this sport, and wheels were added to the sleds to allow warm-weather riding.

In the 1800s, the ice slides moved to France. The warmer climate required some adjustment in thinking. Closely spaced rollers, like warehouse conveyors, were developed. The first wheeled coaster in Paris was opened in 1804. It was called the Russian Mountains. On this monster, small carriages whipped down a steep wooden hill. Many of the carriages jumped the track and caused injuries. As the years passed, more sophisticated rides were developed.

Roller coasters come in many shapes and sizes today. They are found worldwide. Many people have ridden at least one and have certainly experienced the ride secondhand through television or video. Each rolling monster is out there just waiting for the chance to accelerate your heart rate.

Use the passage (page 23) to answer the following questions.

1. What would be an appropriate title for this article? _____

_____

2. What was the author's purpose in writing the first paragraph? _____

_____

3. Locate four descriptive verbs in the passage. Use each verb in a sentence of your own. Underline the verb in each sentence. _____

_____

_____

_____

_____

4. Locate four descriptive adjectives in the passage. Use each adjective in a sentence of your own. Underline the adjective in each sentence. _____

_____

_____

_____

_____

Number the events below to put them in the correct sequence.

_____ Wheels were added to ice-slide sleds.

_____ Russian Mountains was opened in Paris.

_____ Sophisticated rides were developed.

_____ In Russia, people made hills of wooden frames and covered them with hard-packed snow.

_____ Ice slides moved to France.

_____ Colorful lanterns allowed night sledding in St. Petersburg.

Reporting Out

Circle *fact* or *opinion* for each statement. Highlight words that helped you decide which statements were opinions.

Report Card Comments

fact opinion	**1.** Gabe handed in 15 out of 17 possible homework assignments.
fact opinion	**2.** Talia completed an incredible science project.
fact opinion	**3.** Uma is a great reader.
fact opinion	**4.** Jesse read 32 books during this grading period.
fact opinion	**5.** Ralph's art project is gorgeous.
fact opinion	**6.** Carmon is a great author.
fact opinion	**7.** Jean's average test score is 97%.
fact opinion	**8.** Pilar is an excellent mathematician.
fact opinion	**9.** Maya's lab reports are detailed and accurate.
fact opinion	**10.** It is fun to work with Jamal; he has a great attitude.
fact opinion	**11.** Zack is reading, with comprehension, at a level of 5.89.
fact opinion	**12.** Lonnie's world map is accurate, neat, and easy to read.

13. Write a statement of fact. _____

_____

_____

14. Write an opinion statement. _____

_____

_____

Is That a Fact?

Read each statement. Write *F* next to each fact and *O* next to each opinion. Highlight words that helped you decide which statements were opinions.

_____ **1.** Bamboo is an amazing plant.

_____ **2.** Asthma is a chronic lung condition.

_____ **3.** It is annoying to listen to other people complain.

_____ **4.** Propane is a hydrocarbon that is used for fuel.

_____ **5.** Exercising and eating a balanced diet will help you stay healthy.

_____ **6.** The Tour de France is a nearly 4,000 km bicycle race.

_____ **7.** Pennies are worthless; it costs nearly a penny to make just one of those coins.

_____ **8.** Our galaxy is called the Milky Way.

_____ **9.** Sugar will dissolve in water.

_____ **10.** Autumn is the best time of the year.

_____ **11.** A meteorite is a meteor that strikes Earth's surface.

_____ **12.** Skunks are disgustingly smelly creatures.

_____ **13.** It is difficult to spell words like *recapitulation*, *cipher*, and *ptarmigan*.

_____ **14.** A seismometer is an instrument that measures earthquake activity.

15. Rewrite one opinion statement as a fact._____

_____

_____

16. Rewrite one fact statement as an opinion._____

_____

_____

Microscopic

Read the letter below. Then, follow the directions.

Dear Sierra,

We have been using an electron microscope in science class to look at a lot of incredibly small objects. Ms. Micro has a bunch of really neat equipment that puts the picture up on a screen, in an eerie black and white. We can see loads of teeny-tiny things that hang out right in the room with us.

We saw a lot of things yesterday. First, we saw some flaky stuff. It folded over itself and looked like a bunch of crinkled paper. It was not something I was ever going to go near. Then, we looked at some stringy-looking stuff with bulbous things on the ends. You should have heard the gags when Ms. Micro told us what we were looking at: flaked-off skin and a disgusting skin fungus. She said that it is on our skin all of the time, but when our skin stays wet or moist, it can become a nasty rash, like athlete's foot. Gross! It makes my skin crawl.

We also saw something that looked like a close up of craters on the moon. Some slimy stuff on it looked like a dangerous chemical that a monster has squirted on it. It was an unbrushed tooth with harmful bacteria working to make a cavity. I get shivers thinking of that slime on my teeth.

Finally, Ms. Micro showed us space aliens. They went across the screen one by one, each worse than the one before. They were more gruesome and repulsive than any of the horror films I've watched. They had vacuum-cleaner mouths, horrible jointed weapons attached to their bodies, and holes for shooting acids. Would you believe that they were dust mites, aphids, ladybugs, and ants? It made me never want to touch one of those crawly little things again.

Well, I have to go. Science class is next. I'll let you know what we see today.

Sincerely,

Grace

1. Identify and circle at least 10 opinion words in Grace's letter.

2. Locate two facts in the letter. Write the facts below, leaving out any opinion words.

_____

_____

Stretching It?

Some authors add **fantastic details** to make their writing more interesting. Other authors stick to **reality**. As you read, ask yourself, "Could this really happen?"

Read the passages below. If the statements could really happen, write *R* on the line. Write *F* if fantastic details have been added. Underline the fantastic parts.

_____ **1.** My dog Petey loves to eat ham sandwiches. He's always trying to swipe mine.

_____ **2.** Lana's feet were sore. Walking 2 million miles through the museum in one afternoon was wearing holes in her tennis shoes.

_____ **3.** Brynn's new scissors were sharp. They cut through everything with ease: paper, her desk, and the wall.

_____ **4.** Joanna couldn't wait until her family's new television came. They had built a theater to house the enormous screen since their ceilings were too low.

_____ **5.** Mike hated emptying the dishwasher. Whenever he could, he scooted outside before his mother could remind him of his chore.

_____ **6.** Seth enjoyed spending time with his friend, Ibit. He wished that he could spend time at Ibit's house, but the atmosphere on Jupiter was deadly to humans.

_____ **7.** Haley was in tears. She had fallen and skinned her knee for the second time this week.

_____ **8.** Will was frustrated with his soccer team. They hadn't scored any points for the past three games.

_____ **9.** Luke loved sitting in the hot tub. On a clear night, he could see one or two satellites crossing the sky.

_____ **10.** Sheema was having a hard time walking barefoot across the burning beach sand. She put her toes in the cooling waves to snuff out the flames.

11. Write a statement that is based in reality._____

_____

12. Now, add fantastic details to your statement. _____

_____

Kick the Can

Read the following story that Miguel told his little sister, Ella, about a game of kick the can. He started with the truth and elaborated "just a little." Highlight the fantastic details with yellow.

My friends and I decided to play hide-and-seek. The new kid wanted to play, too. He was Frizorio—he was "it." We soon found out that it was no ordinary game. Anyone who was found was frozen. It started when Frizorio found Theo. He touched Theo, and Theo froze. He was really frozen solid! We were afraid that he would never move again. There he stood in the middle of the yard, just a statue with a startled look on his face, poised to run. One after another, Frizorio caught Ned, Kira, Juan, Vince, Porchia, and Sara. Soon there was a yard full of statues. Only Jon and I were left. Boy, were we scared!

Frizorio called out, "They'll stay this way forever unless you kick the magic can. The can has the power to thaw them and restore their movement."

At just about that time, Frizorio's sister, Westy, came looking for him. Apparently, it was time for supper—probably a magic potion or something. She looked around, disgusted. "Playing that game again, huh?" she said. "It would be nice if you filled them in on the rules before you started. Still have the can in your pocket? Give it to me." Frizorio reluctantly handed over the can. I could tell that he was mad. I was afraid that he was going to turn his sister into a frog or something. She took the can and set it down at the end of the driveway. "There. Now, they at least have a chance."

Jon and I decided that the only chance we had was if we worked together. One of us would distract Frizorio while the other kicked that spell-stopping can. I had to get to the can while Jon distracted Frizorio. We decided to wait until Jon got to the other side of the yard. When he ran out, I went for it. Jon got Frizorio to chase him around the side of the house. I made a mad dash, reaching speeds of 50 miles per hour. It all seemed to happen in slow motion, though. I could see Frizorio out of the corner of my eye. He was in hot pursuit, flying across the yard. I could hear him breathing down my neck. With a final burst of speed, I saved the neighborhood! I kicked the can. A magical note rang out restoring movement to all. I was a hero!

29

If Miguel had stuck to the facts, which statement from each pair below would have been in his story? Circle each **factual** statement.

1. The kids play a game of freeze-tag-style kick the can.

A kid with magical powers had moved into the neighborhood.

2. When the kids are tagged, they have to stop and stand as though they are frozen.

The kids are actually frozen and not able to move.

3. Frizorio has a magic can that he keeps in his pocket.

Frizorio cheats by picking up the can and putting it in his pocket.

4. Miguel is worried that something bad will happen to his sister if she plays the game.

Miguel doesn't want his sister to play and is trying to scare her.

5. Frizorio is the name that they give to the person who is "it."

Frizorio is really the new kid's name.

6. The can is a soda can or an old soup can.

The can is really magic.

7. Frizorio is running across the yard when Miguel reaches the can.

Frizorio is flying through the air when Miguel reaches the can.

8. Frizorio's sister is tired of him using magic without telling his friends.

Frizorio's sister is tired of him cheating; she catches him and makes him stop.

9. Westy is an older sister who thinks that the game is for kids.

Westy is Frizorio's sister who thinks that the game is only for people who can use magic.

10. Miguel runs at speeds of 50 mph or greater.

Miguel runs as fast as he can.

One after Another

Read each paragraph below. Then, answer the questions.

Tien was sitting on the swing. Juan walked up behind him. Juan grabbed the swing in both hands and pulled as he backed up. He pushed as he ran forward, let go of the swing, and ducked under the swing as it soared into the air. Tien rode up into the air, and came whooshing back down. He used his legs to pump and continued swinging in the back and forth arc.

1. What causes Tien to go forward? _____

2. What is the effect of Tien's going forward? _____

Jan set her lunch bag on the bus seat. She turned around to talk to a friend and bumped the bag onto the floor. Her apple rolled four seats forward, and her popcorn spilled into a white puddle. Jan watched as her drink bottle bounced three times and then exploded.

3. What causes Jan's lunch to hit the floor? _____

4. What is the effect of the bottle bouncing three times? _____

Ava desperately wanted a puppy. She wrote a plan for paying for the new pet and caring for it. Then, she demonstrated her responsibility by helping with household chores for a month. Her parents were so impressed that they agreed to the new addition to the household.

5. What causes Ava to write a plan? _____

6. What is the effect of Ava's helping with chores? _____

_____

Write and answer one cause question and one effect question for the following paragraph.

Pablo set his alarm for 7:30 A.M. so that he would have a half hour to finish his homework in the morning. He went to sleep. That night, there was a thunderstorm. The power went out for five minutes and then came back on. The next morning, Pablo's mom called for him at 8:00. Pablo couldn't believe it. His alarm had not gone off. He had to rush to get ready for school and finish his homework.

7. _____

_____

8. _____

_____

Friendly Conversation

> In a **conversation**, what one person says affects the other person's response. There is a cause-and-effect relationship.

Read Riley's one-sided dialogue below. Think about what Tyler would say based upon what Riley says. Then, fill in the missing dialogue.

Riley: Hi, Tyler. Will you help me with this math problem?

Tyler: _____

Riley: Yeah, I'd love to play tag when we're finished.

Tyler: _____

Riley: It's this one: 3,405 minus 2,673.

Tyler: _____

Riley: Well, I keep getting 1,272 as the answer. But, when I add it to 2,673, I get 3,945—not 3,405. I know that it's wrong.

Tyler: _____

Riley: Yeah, it is frustrating.

Tyler: _____

Riley: Oh, that's right. I can't take 7 from 0 and still get 7.

Tyler: _____

Riley: I know; we won't give up. Can you look over this again?

Tyler: _____

Riley: The hundreds?

Tyler: _____

Riley: I see. I can't subtract 6 from the 3 that I have left from regrouping the hundreds to the tens. I have to regroup the thousands to the hundreds, also.

Tyler: _____

Riley: Now, I get 732. I can add that to 2,673, and I get 3,405! We did it! Thanks, Tyler.

Tyler: _____

Riley: Yeah, let's put this away and go outside.

Tyler: _____

Riley: Good idea. Let's go get the other guys and then play in your field.

Unfamiliar Words

> The meaning of an unfamiliar word can often be determined by its **context**, or the meanings of the words around it.

Use the context to define each boldfaced word.

1. Carbon dioxide, nitrogen, and oxygen were exhaled from the **fumarole** on the side of the volcano.

   fumarole: _____

2. The huge **sauropod** ate leaves and plants. This dinosaur weighed 16 times more than an elephant.

   sauropod: _____

3. Nina politely asked Alex to move. When he did not respond, she gently **nudged** him with her elbow.

   nudged: _____

4. The greenish slime was a **homogeneous** mixture. We looked at it closely, and it was the same throughout.

   homogeneous: _____

5. The beaver chewed the **limbs** off several trees. It **gnawed** a last branch before dragging all of them one by one into the pond.

   limbs: _____

   gnawed: _____

6. The late students had a **plethora** of excuses. They always had an excessive number of reasons for being **tardy**.

   plethora: _____

   tardy: _____

7. The cello soloist played the **ritornello**, a short **recurrent** instrumental passage, for the third time during the arrangement.

   ritornello: _____

   recurrent: _____

8. **Atoms**, the smallest building blocks of matter, are made up of **protons** (positively charged particles), **electrons** (negatively charged particles), and **neutrons** (particles with no charge).

   atoms: _____

   protons: _____

   electrons: _____

   neutrons: _____

Summer Bridge Reading RB-904096

Wise Words

> A **proverb** is a wise or thoughtful saying.

Match each proverb with the best meaning.

A. A friend in need is a friend indeed.

B. Don't change horses in midstream.

C. Don't cry over spilled milk.

D. Don't count your chickens before they hatch.

E. The grass is always greener on the other side.

F. Half a loaf is better than none.

G. Make hay while the sun shines.

H. Many hands make light work.

I. Money burns a hole in your pocket.

J. Time is money.

K. Two heads are better than one.

____ **1.** Do not make plans for something until you actually have it.

____ **2.** Do not change your mind once you've decided how to do something.

____ **3.** Do not procrastinate. Get your work done when you should.

____ **4.** Having part of something is better than not having any of it.

____ **5.** No matter what you have, you always think that what someone else has looks better.

____ **6.** It helps to listen to other people's ideas when you are trying to solve a problem.

____ **7.** You want to spend money before thinking about the best way to spend it.

____ **8.** Things are done quickly and easily when everyone helps.

____ **9.** When someone wants something, he acts like a good friend so that you will help him.

____ **10.** When you make a mistake, forget it and move on.

____ **11.** Value your time. It is worth a lot.

Write two of your own wise sayings below. Explain the meaning of each proverb.

_____

_____

_____

_____

Figures of Speech

An **idiom** is a figure of speech. An **idiomatic phrase** has a different meaning than the literal meaning of the individual words.

Fill in the circle next to the best meaning for the boldfaced idiom.

1. Father asked Yasmin to be quiet while he was on the phone. Wayne was intentionally bothering Yasmin. Mother told Yasmin to ignore Wayne or she would **play right into his hands.**

    A. put his hands on her shoulders

    B. fall into a trap that someone plans for ulterior motives

    C. make noise by playing hand instruments

2. While Wendy was reading her novel, she **ran across** the date when World War II began.

    A. moved quickly across a library

    B. crossed out the dates

    C. happened to find information

3. Adrian thought that he was too old to help with the scavenger hunt. Melinda told him to **let his hair down** and join in the fun.

    A. take his hair out of the rubber band

    B. relax

    C. get his hands out of his hair

4. We could hardly **keep a straight face** when Maddie looked at her four-year-old friend and very seriously said, "I believe that you should act your age."

    A. not laugh or smile

    B. not have any curves or angles

    C. keep the drawing of a face as straight as a ruler

5. Brett did not tell Chelsea the secret, because he did not want her to **let the cat out of the bag.**

    A. tell the secret

    B. let the kitten (who was a secret) out of his backpack

    C. rip a hole in the tote bag

Idioms

Use the clues below to unscramble the idioms. Write the idioms on the lines.

1. If someone gives you a bike, don't complain that the back tire is flat.

   gift mouth look the horse in don't a

   _____

2. If you use your brother's old binder instead of buying a new one, you can save enough money for a computer game faster.

   is penny penny a saved a earned

   _____

3. If you fail the test by just one point, you have still failed the test.

   a good mile as as miss is a

   _____

4. If your best friend loses a CD that you loaned her, you shouldn't let it ruin your friendship.

   make out molehill don't a of mountain a

   _____

5. The first grader next door spent his birthday money on candy. He ate it all in one night and became sick.

   parted money and a soon his are fool

   _____

Extra! Dare to dream! Unscramble the following saying.

hchit ruyo ngawo ot a rtsa

___ ___ ___ ___ ___   ___ ___ ___ ___   ___ ___ ___ ___ ___

___ ___   ___ ___   ___ ___ ___ ___ ___.

Awesome Analogies

An **analogy** is a comparison or relationship between two or more things that may otherwise not be alike. To complete an analogy, you must first determine what the relationship between the words is. Then, determine which word could be added to keep the relationship the same. The relationships in the examples below use synonyms, antonyms, and homophones to demonstrate analogies.

Examples: Alone is to solo as ocean is to sea. (synonyms)
Rear is to front as back is to stomach. (antonyms).
Week is to weak as hour is to our. (homophones).

Circle the letter next to each correct answer.

1. Telescope is to star as microscope is to _____.
   A. planet   **B.** glass   **C.** cell

2. Omniscient is to knowledge as omnipotent is to _____.
   A. hope   **B.** power   **C.** fear

3. In is to import as out is to _____.
   A. exit   **B.** exult   **C.** export

4. Assertive is to passive as definite is to _____.
   A. vague   **B.** exact   **C.** define

5. Funny is to hilarious as good is to _____.
   A. sullen   **B.** benevolent   **C.** relentless

6. Silly is to ridiculous as love is to _____.
   A. fear   **B.** adore   **C.** tolerate

7. Reveal is to divulge as hide is to _____.
   A. discover   **B.** imagine   **C.** conceal

8. Observe is to observation as condense is to _____.
   A. condenser   **B.** condensation   **C.** watch

9. Piece is to fragment as daydream is to _____.
   A. reverie   **B.** night   **C.** deem

10. Gratitude is to ingratitude as grateful is to _____.
    A. ungrateful   **B.** thankful   **C.** gratefully

Milkweed

Read the text and answer the questions below.

Maddie stood by the side of the road. She turned over yet another pale green leaf. No caterpillar. In her other hand, covered with sticky, milky fluid, was a nearly empty ice cream bucket. One lone black-, yellow-, and white-striped caterpillar was monotonously eating larger and larger swaths out of the leaf on the milkweed stem that she had placed in there for its lunch. At this rate, she would need more leaves before leaving for school in the morning. Maddie looked up. She saw her friend Jade approaching. Jade parked her bike. "What are you looking for?" she asked.

"I promised my teacher that I would bring five monarch caterpillars for our first science lesson this year. I've found only one so far." Jade put down her kickstand and began to help Maddie. She looked on several milkweed leaves and then moved over to look at the stem of a dandelion.

"Don't look there," said Maddie. "Monarch caterpillars eat only milkweed leaves. I've looked over this patch twice and can't find any more."

"No problem," Jade replied. "There is a huge patch of milkweed behind my house."

1. What is the setting? _____

2. Who are the characters? Circle the name of each character once in the story. _____

_____

3. What is the problem? _____

_____

4. What is your predicted solution? _____

_____

Highlight details in the story that helped you think of a solution.

5. Write two facts about monarch caterpillars. _____

_____

© Rainbow Bridge Publishing

Getting the Setting

> The **setting** includes both the time and place.

Identify each setting in the paragraphs. Write the place and circle the time. Highlight the words that helped you find the answers.

1. Heath studied the *Tyrannosaurus rex* display at the Field Museum in Chicago. He filled in several answers on his field trip questionnaire.

   Where?_____

   When?   in the past   in the present   in the future

2. Jill was exhausted. She woke at sunup to cook breakfast over the campfire and help load the wagon. Then, she got in line with the other wagons. Eight hours later, she was still sitting on the buckboard trying to guide the oxen. She hoped that the place called California was worth the three-month trip.

   Where?_____

   When?   in the past   in the present   in the future

3. Kayla flopped on her bed. She couldn't wait to get her gumbawa. It was the best pet in the universe! Her brother Kyle had promised to bring her one. She would be the first person in Idaho to have one. Kyle's hyperspace transport from Uranna Four was due back on Earth this week.

   Where?_____

   When?   in the past   in the present   in the future

4. Tyrone watched the eagle through his binoculars. He was glad that he had the weekend to research his spring project on Oregon eagles. He observed the female eagle return to the nest at the top of the enormous pine with food for the young one.

   Where?_____

   When?   in the past   in the present   in the future

5. Luis sat at his desk, bored. He had heard the history lesson about the world wars of the 1900s many times. After all, that had happened more than 600 years ago.

   Where?_____

   When?   in the past   in the present   in the future

Within Time

> A **time frame** is a specific period of time. It tells you when an event happened or when it will take place.
>
> **Example:**
>
> in the past: Willow rode the stagecoach to New Mexico.
>
> in the present: Willow rode in the van to the store.
>
> in the future: Willow rode the rocket to Jupiter.

Read each sentence to determine the time frame. Write *past*, *present*, or *future* to show when the action happened. Highlight the word or words that helped you find your answer. Then, rewrite the sentence so that the action happens in the other two time frames. Write *past*, *present*, or *future* for the rewritten sentences.

1. _____ Jayla used her computer to write the story.

_____ _____

_____ _____

2. _____ Urg paid for the raw dinosaur meat with four rocks.

_____ _____

_____ _____

3. _____ Erin toasted her grilled cheese sandwich on the stove.

_____ _____

_____ _____

4. _____ Paolo loved his virtual reality novel. He could actually smell and feel the terrain of Yerba, Mars.

_____ _____

_____ _____

5. _____ Galia pulled her furs closer. The sun's first rays would soon wake the family.

_____ _____

_____ _____

What's the Problem?

Read the paragraph. Write the problem on the line. Then, pick one of the problems. Write a good solution to the problem on the lines below.

1. Porchia stared at the massive mess in her room. It had to be clean before she could leave for the movie. "Oh, why didn't I start this on Monday?" she thought. "The movie starts in two hours. I'll never finish in time!"

   Problem: _____

2. "Look at that!" yelled Tom. Rob grabbed his arm and started to run toward the stairs. "We should not have dared him to do it," said Rob. Tony was soaring down the stairs' handrail on his skateboard.

   Problem: _____

3. Darryl wanted to be in the school play. Tryouts were Thursday after school. The bus would be gone by the time tryouts were finished, and neither of Darryl's parents would be able to pick him up.

   Problem: _____

4. Ana grabbed her favorite sweater from the drawer. She started to button it up. Suddenly, a button popped off the sweater and dropped onto the floor with a clunk.

   Problem: _____

5. Eric wanted a new MP3 player. He thought that he would get one for his birthday, but he didn't. He received $40 instead. The MP3 player that he wanted cost $87.

   Problem: _____

6. **Solution:** _____

   _____

   _____

   _____

   _____

   _____

My New Companion

Read the passage.

I remember the day we met. It was my ninth birthday. My mom and I were pulling into the driveway when I saw it, my new companion, standing next to my dad. It was awesome! Instantly, I fell in love with the worn, yellow seat and the polished chrome handlebars that gleamed in the afternoon sun. My eyes lit up, and without hesitation, I jumped out of the car and climbed aboard.

It took me a while to feel completely comfortable with my new companion, but before two weeks had passed, we were inseparable. Every day, we would ride, rain or shine. It was on one of those days that we faced our biggest challenge.

It was a bright, sunny day. My companion and I were cruising along a relatively flat and well-paved street two blocks from my house when we encountered a group of boys who had set up a ramp. I stopped pedaling and paused to watch as the boys took turns riding their bikes up the ramp, which propelled them straight into the air before they landed back on the pavement with a loud clank and clatter. The point was to fly as high into the air as possible.

When a few of the boys in the group finally noticed me, they signaled for me to come over. "Hey there," said a red-headed kid with many freckles as I approached the group, "why don't you give it a try?" The thought of riding up a ramp hadn't crossed my mind until then, but the redhead persisted, so I lined myself up to take the plunge.

My palms began to sweat, and my heart pounded as I contemplated the possibility that I might crash. The more I thought about what I was doing, the more frightened I became. Knowing that I would become completely paralyzed with fear if I didn't do something soon, I climbed onto the yellow seat, grabbed the handlebars, and let myself go. Without thinking, I started pedaling faster and faster, and before I knew it, I launched into the sky!

It took nearly six weeks for my broken arm to heal. I still went to watch the boys ride their bikes up the ramp. I even made a whole new group of friends, who all signed my cast. The doctor let me keep it as a reminder to be careful.

The minute that I had that cast taken off, I went back to try that jump again. With all of the practice that I've had now, that ramp is no problem. I discovered that whether you're learning to ride a bike, meeting new friends, or taking on a new challenge, overcoming your fear is the first step. Once you do, there's very little that can stop you from achieving your goal!

My New Companion

Answer the following questions using information from the story (page 42).

1. What is the main idea of the story?
   A. Learning to ride a bike is fun.
   B. It is great to receive presents from parents.
   C. It is good to overcome fear.
   D. A companion, like a dog, is great.

2. What is a synonym for the word *companion*?
   A. bike
   B. enemy
   C. parent
   D. partner

3. Which one of the following statements is an opinion, not a fact?
   A. The writer was given a bike for his ninth birthday.
   B. Bikes with yellow seats are the best.
   C. The writer's companion is a bike.
   D. The bike has a worn, yellow seat.

4. Which of the following events happened last?
   A. It took nearly six weeks for the writer's broken arm to heal.
   B. Instantly, the writer fell in love with the worn, yellow seat and the polished chrome handlebars.
   C. The writer's palms began to sweat, and his heart pounded.
   D. The writer and his companion were cruising along.

5. What can you infer happened when the boy jumped the ramp for the first time?
   A. At the last minute, he was too scared to ride up the ramp.
   B. He crashed when he landed.
   C. He flew so high that all of the other boys were jealous.
   D. He broke his bike when he landed.

Go, Bones!

Read the passage below.

Most preteens do not worry about what their bodies will be like when they turn 40 or 50. That seems like such a long way away! Yet, there are some very simple things that can be done before the age of 18 that will have a huge impact on life after 50. It is as simple as exercising, eating right, and getting plenty of calcium and vitamin D, which is needed for calcium absorption.

So, what's the big deal? The problem is osteoporosis—a big word that means bones are losing mass and are more apt to break or fracture. Osteoporosis can even cause collapsed vertebrae, resulting in incredible back pain and spinal deformities, like a rounded back. Osteoporosis poses a serious risk for around 55% of 50-year-old and older Americans. More than 20 million Americans and 1.4 million Canadians suffer from this condition.

Osteoporosis cannot be cured. It can be treated, but not always successfully. The best way to take care of it is to prevent it. The best time to prevent osteoporosis is before the age of 18. From birth to the late teens, people build their greatest amount of bone mass. This is the time when dietary calcium—from food, not pills—directly results in bones growing to their maximum density. If bone mass is not built during this time, it cannot be "caught up" later.

The problem is that many children are not getting enough calcium in their diets. Milk and other dairy products are rich in calcium. Several studies have shown that girls and boys who drink a lot of soft drinks and fruit beverages tend to drink less milk. Other studies have shown that cola and caffeinated beverages leach calcium out of the bones, which means that more calcium is needed to compensate. Depending on the amount of caffeine ingested, anywhere from one to five servings of calcium could be leached from the bones each day.

Most adults need about 1000 mg of dietary calcium per day, without drinking cola; children need slightly more. People under 18 years old need the equivalent of four to five glasses of milk each day. For those who don't like milk, the good news is that calcium can also be found in other foods, like yogurt, cheese, green leafy vegetables, and broccoli. In fact, if you start checking labels, you will be surprised where calcium shows up.

Other preventative measures include regular exercise, a balanced diet, and not smoking. You have the power to take preventative measures now. Armed with knowledge, you can have a direct impact on what your own life will be like many years from now.

Go, Bones!

Answer each of the following questions and underline your answers in the passage (page 44).

1. What is osteoporosis? _____

    _____

2. List two possible consequences of a person having osteoporosis.

    _____

3. Why should kids be concerned about osteoporosis? _____

    _____

    _____

4. When is the most bone mass grown? _____

5. Why is milk important to this issue? _____

6. What can you eat if you do not like to drink milk? _____

7. What effect do caffeinated beverages have on the bones? _____ _____

    _____

8. What, besides calcium, will strengthen your bones and help prevent osteoporosis?

    _____

9. Evaluate your own lifestyle. What can you do to help your bones? _____

    _____

    _____

Babe Didrikson Zaharias

Read the passage below.

Mildred Ella "Babe" Didriksen was born in Port Arthur, Texas, in 1911. She said that she received her nickname after hitting five home runs in a baseball game. Some biographers have noted that her mother, a Norwegian immigrant, called her "Min Babe" as a nickname. As an adult, Babe changed the spelling of her last name to make it sound more Norwegian. In 1938, she married a professional wrestler named George Zaharias.

One of the greatest female athletes of all time, Babe competed in sports throughout her life. Women were not allowed to play many sports in her time, so she took every chance she had to play and compete. Babe was voted the Woman Athlete of the First Half of the 20th Century in a poll. She was also named the Woman Athlete of the Year in 1931, 1945, 1946, 1947, 1950, and 1954.

Best known today as a golfer, she knew little about golf growing up in Beaumont, Texas. In fact, she had gained world fame in track and field and All-American status in basketball before she took up golf. She also mastered tennis, played organized baseball and softball, and was an expert diver, roller skater, and bowler. In track and field, she either held or tied the world record in four events—the javelin throw, 80-meter hurdles, high jump, and long jump—and won two gold medals and one silver medal in the 1932 Olympics.

Already famous, Babe began concentrating on golf in 1935 at the suggestion of sportswriter Grantland Rice. For a time, she was not allowed to play in amateur golf tournaments because she was earning too much money playing basketball and baseball. She played in her first golf tournament a year after learning the rules of the game of golf. In 1946 and 1947, she won 17 amateur golf tournaments in a row.

As a professional golfer, she was a founder and a charter member of the Ladies Professional Golf Association (LPGA). She later became a member of the Golf Hall of Fame. Babe always loved playing sports, and she really loved winning. She had to work hard for her accomplishments, but her hard work paid off for her and other women. Today, it is much easier for girls to play any sport that they want to play. Babe, and other women like her, showed the world that women can be professional athletes, too!

Babe Didrikson Zaharias

Answer the following questions about the passage (page 46).

1. What was Babe's favorite thing to do?
   A. play baseball, basketball, and golf
   B. play baseball and basketball
   C. play any sport
   D. play tennis and golf

2. Where was Babe from?
   A. Texas
   B. Oklahoma
   C. Colorado
   D. Mississippi

3. What title did she receive six different years?
   A. Olympic Athlete of the Year
   B. World's Best Female Athlete
   C. Woman Athlete of the Year
   D. Professional Woman Golfer

4. Where did Babe grow up?
   A. Port Arthur, Texas
   B. Austin, Texas
   C. Beaumont, Texas
   D. Dallas, Texas

5. What medals did she receive in the 1932 Olympics?
   A. two gold and one silver
   B. two gold and two silver
   C. three gold and one silver
   D. two gold and no silver

6. Which of the following sports is Babe best known for today?
   A. basketball
   B. golf
   C. tennis
   D. track

7. In your own words, explain how playing sports is different today than it was 60 years ago for female athletes.

   _____

   _____

   _____

   _____

   _____

   _____

   _____

Summer Bridge Reading RB-904096

Water around Us

> **Study guides** and **notes** can help you prepare for a test because they highlight important information that you may need to know.

- Water is found in three states: solid, liquid, and gas.
    solid: ice (frozen water), glaciers (rivers of ice), icebergs (floating pieces of glaciers),
        frost (ice crystals on objects)
    liquid: rivers, runoff (flows across land), lakes, oceans, ground water (in or below soil)
    gas: water vapor, steam

- Water as a gas is called water vapor

- Water is continually changing states. Each change is a part of the never-ending water cycle: evaporation, condensation, precipitation, and storage (reservoir).

- Evaporation is the change from a liquid state to a gas state. Water on the surface changes to water vapor when the air becomes warmer.

- Three things can help speed up evaporation: heat, wind, and increased surface area.

- Condensation occurs when water changes from a gas back to a liquid.

- In the water cycle, condensation refers to clouds and fog. Clouds form when water vapor rises and cools, condensing on very small particles in the air, like dust. In cold air, the water vapor changes to small ice crystals. Clouds are formed from millions of these drops or crystals.

- Fog is a cloud near the ground.

- Precipitation is water that falls from clouds.
    rain: liquid water that falls when the air is warmer than 0°C (32°F)
    snow: ice crystals that fall when the air is cooler than 0°C (32°F)
    sleet: frozen rain
    hail: small spheres formed from many layers of ice

- Storage, or reservoir, is a place that stores water. Examples include lakes, rivers, ground water, plants, glaciers, pools, water towers, and swamps.

- Most of the liquid water on Earth is salt water.

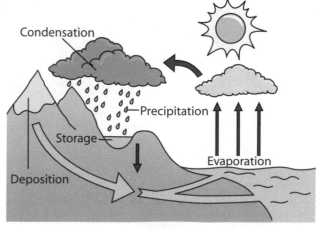

Water around Us

Match the terms with the descriptions. Write the letter on each line.

_____ A place that stores water

_____ It moves through soil and rocks.

_____ It shows how water is always changing states.

_____ Rain, sleet, and snow

_____ How clouds are formed

_____ Changing from liquid water to water vapor

_____ A large tank used as a reservoir

_____ A large river of ice

_____ Water that flows across land

_____ A large block of ice floating in the ocean

A. evaporation

B. iceberg

C. runoff

D. condensation

E. reservoir

F. ground water

G. water tower

H. water cycle

I. precipitation

J. glacier

Answer the following questions.

1. In what three states can water be found on Earth?

_____ _____ _____

2. Where can liquid water be found on Earth? Give three examples.

_____ _____ _____

3. What kinds of precipitation can be found at these temperatures?

-2°C _____   **15°C** _____

4. List four different uses of water.

_____   _____

_____   _____

5. Is most of the liquid water on Earth fresh water or salt water? _____

6. What three things can help speed up evaporation?

_____ _____ _____

Summer Bridge Reading RB-904096

Water around Us (continued)

Circle the letter next to the answer.

7. Water that falls from clouds is
   A. condensation.   B. precipitation.   C. evaporation.

8. A cloud very close to the ground is
   A. sleet.   B. hail.   C. fog.

9. Which of the following does not speed up evaporation?
   A. wind   B. decreased surface area   C. heat

10. Water vapor may condense to liquid water when it
    A. becomes cooler.   B. becomes warmer.   C. evaporates.

11. Evaporation takes place where water is
    A. in the air.   B. on the surface.   C. deep below the surface.

12. Ice crystals that form on objects are called
    A. snow.   B. frost.   C. sleet.

13. Frozen rain is called
    A. hail.   B. sleet.   C. clouds.

14. Precipitation that falls as liquid water is
    A. hail.   B. sleet.   C. rain.

15. Liquid water evaporates when the air
    A. becomes cooler.   B. becomes warmer.   C. condenses.

Answer the following questions in complete sentences.

A. What is water vapor? _____

B. How do clouds form? _____

_____

_____

Rocks in the Head

> The **main idea** identifies the main point (or points) in a passage. Each paragraph of a passage has a **topic sentence**, which tells the main idea of the paragraph and supports the main idea of the passage. All of the details in a paragraph are clues to help you understand the topic sentence and main idea. These clues are called **supporting details.**

All four topic sentences below refer to the same main idea: rocks. The supporting details are listed separately. Match each detail to the appropriate topic sentence.

1. Rocks can be found in many places.

   _____   _____   _____

2. Rocks have many uses.

   _____   _____   _____

3. There are three different types of rocks.

   _____   _____   _____

4. Various forces weather rocks.

   _____   _____   _____

A. Water washes away bits and pieces of rock.

B. Sedimentary rock is formed underwater as millions of years worth of mud, pebbles, and other objects are pressed together and solidified.

C. Ground rocks are mixed together with an adhering agent to make concrete.

D. Mountains are comprised of enormous sheets of rock.

E. Bedrock is located below soil.

F. Bedrock provides stability for homes and other structures.

G. Changes in temperature cause cracks to develop in rocks.

H. Gemstones in rocks are used for jewelry, decoration, and cutting tools.

I. Igneous rock is produced from hardened magma and lava.

J. Many rocks found beneath the ocean depths are a result of underwater volcanoes.

K. Wind kicks up sand and other materials and sandblasts standing rock structures.

L. Metamorphic rock is igneous or sedimentary rock that has been changed by a combination of heat and pressure.

Summer Bridge Reading RB-904096

Infectious Disease

Read the passage.

Infectious viral diseases can be as frightening today as they were in the past, before they had been studied and identified. Viral diseases are contagious. When they are not contained, they can become health hazards. An **epidemic** is an infectious viral disease that affects a large number of people. The infection spreads outside a limited group and lasts for a long time. The plague, or "black death," spread through fleas that were infected by black rats and is one example of an epidemic. A **pandemic** is more widespread than an epidemic. A pandemic is an infectious viral disease that is established around the world. The spread of smallpox among Native Americans during the 16th century is an example of a pandemic. An **endemic** is an infectious disease that is present in certain areas or populations all of the time. It is often caused by an abnormality in plant or animal life exclusive to that area. Malaria, which is transported by the mosquito in tropical and subtropical countries, is one example of an endemic. Through time, scientists have developed immunizations and medications that help fight some of these diseases and treat their symptoms. But, for many of the diseases, there is still no cure.

Write the topic of the passage on the line below. Write the main idea in the top oval. Write three major details in the next set of ovals. Write minor details in the rectangles.

Topic: _____

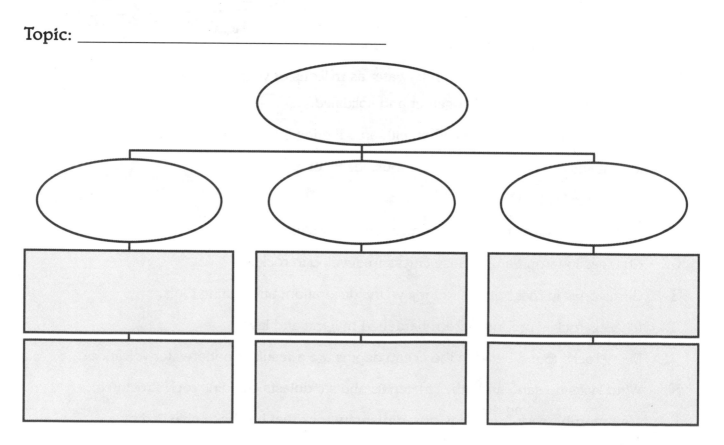

Turn Up the Power

Read the passage.

The ability to do work is called energy. Machines need energy, or fuel, to work. This energy can come from many sources. Fossil fuels, like coal, gas, and oil, are one important source of energy. They come from the earth and are used to fuel power plants, automobiles, and other machines. Another source of energy is wind. Wind can power windmills. It can also be converted into electricity, push gears to grind grains, or be used to pump water. Water is also a key source of energy. Dams are used to harness energy from rivers and convert it into electricity. Scientists are researching the possibility of using ocean waves and tides for energy. Finally, there is the sun, or solar energy. Solar cells can turn sunlight to electricity, which can then be used to power cars and electrical devices and heat homes. Although fossil fuels are currently used the most, other energy sources are becoming more commonly used and research is being done to make those energy sources more effective and economical.

Write the topic and main idea on the lines below. Then, list four major supporting details. Choose two minor supporting details for each major detail and list them.

Topic: _____

Main idea: _____

1. Major supporting detail: _____

    A. Minor supporting detail: _____

    B. Minor supporting detail: _____

2. Major supporting detail: _____

    A. Minor supporting detail: _____

    B. Minor supporting detail: _____

3. Major supporting detail: _____

    A. Minor supporting detail: _____

    B. Minor supporting detail: _____

4. Major supporting detail: _____

    A. Minor supporting detail: _____

    B. Minor supporting detail: _____

    Summer Bridge Reading RB-904096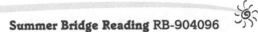

Vertebrates

Read the passage.

Vertebrates are animals that have backbones. Animals that do not have backbones are called invertebrates, or "not vertebrates." There are five different kinds of vertebrates: amphibians, birds, fish, mammals, and reptiles. Each type has distinct characteristics. Some are warm-blooded, while others are cold-blooded. Body coverings, habitats, methods of reproduction, and methods of breathing differ from one to another. The one characteristic that all vertebrates—no matter what shape or size—share is a skeletal structure with a backbone.

Amphibians are cold-blooded, skin-covered vertebrates. They have two distinct parts to their life cycles. The adult female lays jellylike eggs that hatch into water creatures. Infant and juvenile amphibians have gills and spend their time in fluid environments. When they become adults, a transition is made—gills make way for lungs—and they spend most of their time on land. Although adult amphibians must breathe air, many often need water to stay moist. Frogs and salamanders are common examples of amphibians.

Like amphibians, birds can live around water. In fact, penguins are more comfortable in water than on land. Some of these feathered creatures, like kingfishers, even eat amphibians. Birds also live on nearly every type of land feature, and the majority of birds spend much of their time airborne. Not all birds fly, but all birds are covered with feathers. Unlike amphibians, birds are warm-blooded. They breathe with lungs from the moment that they hatch from brittle-shelled eggs. When they are born, baby birds are helpless. Without parental care, both while in the egg and after hatching, they will not survive.

Fish are lifelong water creatures. These cold-blooded animals are covered with scales and use gills to extract oxygen from the water. Most fish, like salmon, come from jellylike eggs, but a few, such as guppies, develop inside the mother and are born alive. Fish generally do not care for their young.

Mammals are the only vertebrates whose females produce milk to feed their young. Nearly all mammals give birth to live young. They breathe with lungs and are warm-blooded, and most are covered with hair or fur. Because they are warm-blooded, mammals must make their own heat, which requires additional energy and fuel in the form of food. Mammals have developed many ways to retain heat, such as thicker hair and fur in the winter months, layers of fat under the skin, and, in the case of humans, artificial coverings like clothing. Other examples of mammals include seals, rats, kangaroos, tigers, elephants, and dogs.

Although most mammals are land creatures, there is a group of ocean-dwelling mammals. Many of these mammals are members of the whale family, such as orcas, porpoises, humpbacks, and dolphins. They live in a fluid environment and can hold their breath for long periods of time, but they, too, have lungs and must surface to breathe.

Reptiles are the final group of vertebrates. They are cold-blooded like amphibians and fish. They also lay eggs. Reptiles are covered with scales; some scales form shells, like those of the turtle and tortoise groups. Reptiles lay leathery eggs, and they breathe with lungs. Turtles, alligators, and crocodiles spend much of their time in the water, but they are often found resting on logs or on shore, warming themselves in the sun.

Write the main idea in the top oval below. Write the five major details in the next set of ovals. Finally, write three minor details that support each of the five major details in the rectangles.

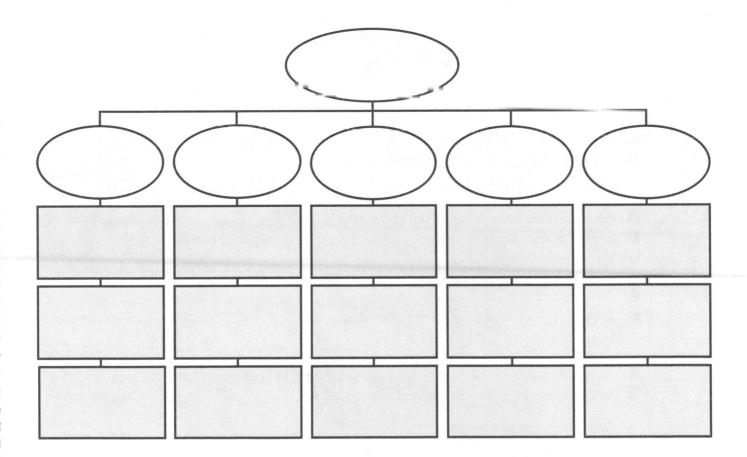

What do you know about asthma? Before you read the passage on pages 57 and 58, read each pair of statements below. Circle the letter next to the statement that you predict is true based on your prior knowledge. Then, read the passage on the following two pages. Review your choices. Write *V* beside each verified answer. Write the number of the paragraph that contains the answer.

1._____ **A.** Asthma is not contagious. It is a chronic lung condition.
       B. Asthma is contagious. It is caused by bacteria or a virus.

       Answer found in paragraph: _____

2._____ **A.** Asthma can be cured.
       B. Asthma can be controlled by taking medications and avoiding triggers.

       Answer found in paragraph: _____

3._____ **A.** When a trigger is present, tight, mucus-filled bronchi will not let oxygen into the lungs.
       B. When a trigger is present, tight, mucus-filled bronchi trap carbon dioxide in the lungs.

       Answer found in paragraph:_____

4._____ **A.** All people with asthma have allergies.
       B. Some people with allergies have asthma.

       Answer found in paragraph: _____

5._____ **A.** Anyone can develop asthma.
       B. Asthmatics are born with asthma.

       Answer found in paragraph:_____

6._____ **A.** An asthmatic always has trouble breathing.
       B. An asthmatic can have trouble breathing when a trigger is present.

       Answer found in paragraph:_____

7._____ **A.** All asthmatics have the same triggers.
       B. Triggers are different for each asthmatic.

       Answer found in paragraph:_____

8._____ **A.** Asthmatics can do all the things you do as long as they monitor their breathing.
       B. Asthmatics can never run, exercise, or play sports.

       Answer found in paragraph: _____

9._____ **A.** Asthmatics go to the hospital each time they have trouble breathing.
       B. Asthmatics can usually take care of their asthma from home, working with their doctors

       Answer found in paragraph: _____

Asthma

Read the passage.

You just found out that your friend has asthma. All sorts of scary questions are running through your mind: Can I catch it? Can my friend still do "normal" things? Is it safe to be around my friend? Will my friend spend a lot of time indoors or in the hospital?

First, asthma is not contagious. You cannot catch it from someone else. It is not passed on by bacteria or a virus, like the flu, strep throat, or a cold. Bacteria or a virus can, however, trigger asthma symptoms in someone who already has asthma. Anyone can develop asthma, including children and adults. There is some evidence that the tendency to develop asthma may be hereditary, or passed on by parents, just like hair color or body size.

What is asthma? Asthma is a chronic condition of two of the body's vital organs. These vital organs are the lungs. Asthma cannot be cured, but it can be managed with medications and by avoiding triggers. Asthma is an ongoing lung condition.

Understanding how the lungs work can help you understand what asthma is. The lungs are made up of bronchi, which are interconnecting passageways that let oxygen and carbon dioxide pass between the body and the outside air. The bronchi branch off into smaller passageways called bronchioles. This entire system is often called the brachial tree. The bronchi are covered with cilia, which are small, hairlike projections that use mucus to sweep dust and other particles out of the lungs.

Asthma is a lung condition that acts differently with different people. However, all asthmatics, or people with asthma, have oversensitive lungs. They have problems when the muscles surrounding the bronchi squeeze too tightly and the brachial tree produces too much mucus. This can make it hard for the asthmatic person to breathe, and it can also make her wheeze, or sound raspy when she breathes. Because the airways are tighter and contain extra mucus, carbon dioxide gets trapped in the lower parts of the brachial tree, which results in a smaller area of the lungs being used for breathing. When oxygen is brought into the lungs, a smaller part of the lungs is able to absorb it and bring it to the body. The problem is not taking in oxygen: it is releasing the trapped carbon dioxide. The good news is that the lungs do not behave this way all of the time—only when a trigger is present.

When an asthma attack occurs, a trigger causes the airways to constrict, or get smaller, and produce more mucus, trapping carbon dioxide in the lungs. Triggers are different for each asthmatic and can include allergens, irritants, viruses or bacteria, exercise, or stress. Just because a person has an allergy does not mean he has or will have asthma, just as a person who has asthma does not necessarily have allergies.

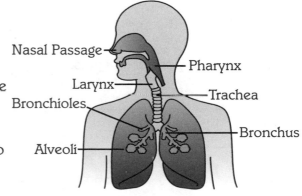

Nasal Passage — Pharynx — Larynx — Trachea — Bronchioles — Bronchus — Alveoli

Summer Bridge Reading RB-904096

Asthmatics can take care of their asthma at home if they work with their doctors. An asthma attack does not have to involve a trip to the hospital. Many asthmatics have emergency medications and equipment at home, such as peak flow meters, inhalers, pills, and steroids. An acute attack occurs when an asthmatic cannot control her breathing. When this happens, a trip to the emergency room and a short stay in the hospital may be necessary.

Asthmatics can lead normal lives. They can play sports, travel, and do all sorts of fun things. They do, however, need to be aware of their own triggers. Different things trigger asthma in different patients. It is not the same for everyone. Knowledge, the correct medications and equipment, and a good working relationship with a doctor are an asthmatic's best tools.

Answer the questions using information from the passage.

A. What does the word *chronic* mean in paragraph 3? _____

_____

Highlight the answer in the passage with yellow.

B. What are bronchi? _____

_____

Highlight the answer in the passage with green.

C. How do bronchi affect an asthmatic? _____

_____

D. What is a trigger? _____

_____

Highlight the answer in the passage with blue.

E. List four possible triggers.

_____   _____

_____   _____

Great Lakes

Read the passage.

The Great Lakes, located in North America, are the largest bodies of freshwater in the world. It is generally believed that they were made by glaciers that once covered the area. As the glaciers retreated, they gouged the land, melted, and filled the five Great Lakes, as well as many other smaller lakes and rivers in the area.

Today, the Great Lakes are shared by two countries: the United States and Canada. The lakes provide people in the area with freshwater for drinking and for use in their homes. The lakes also assist many power plants and manufacturing companies. Recreation and transportation are two additional benefits. These lakes are home to numerous freshwater fish, like salmon, perch, trout, and walleye.

Lake Superior is the the largest freshwater lake in the world and the deepest of the five lakes. Lake Superior also lies the farthest north of the Great Lakes. This lake is cold year-round and can develop violent storms. Because of this, many ships lie at the bottom of Lake Superior, including the famous *Edmund Fitzgerald*. The Soo Canals, completed in 1855, connect Lake Superior to Lake Huron, which is more than 20 feet (6.1 m) lower than Lake Superior. The canals were built to transport large ships and goods.

Lake Huron is named for an American Indian tribe that once lived along its shores. This lake has more islands than any other four Great Lakes. Most of these islands are nearer to the Canadian border than the Michigan border. Lake Huron touches Lake Superior at the Soo Canals, Lake Michigan at the Straits of Mackinac, and Lake Erie to the south.

Lake Michigan is the only Great Lake located entirely within the United States. Lake Michigan borders Wisconsin, Illinois, Indiana, and Michigan. The rest of the lakes share boundaries with Canada and the United States.

Lake Erie reaches the farthest south of any of the Great Lakes. It is also the shallowest. The most eastern Great Lake is Lake Ontario.

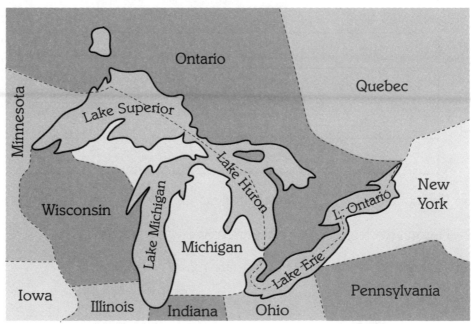

Great Lakes (continued)

Answer the following questions.

1. How were the Great Lakes formed?_____

   _____

   _____

2. How are the Great Lakes used by the people who live on their borders? _____

   _____

   _____

Find the area of each Great Lake. Use the clues below and information in the text and map (page 59) to assist you in completing the matrix.

- The deepest Great Lake is also the largest.

- A lake that connects to another lake at the Straits of Mackinac has the second largest area.

- The shallowest lake is not the smallest in area.

- The lake without a Canadian border has the third largest area.

Area (in square miles)

Great Lakes	7,320	9,910	22,300	23,000	31,700
Erie					
Huron					
Michigan					
Ontario					
Superior					

Lake Erie covers _____ square miles.

Lake Huron covers _____ square miles.

Lake Michigan covers _____ square miles.

Lake Ontario covers _____ square miles.

Lake Superior covers _____ square miles.

Housefly

Read the following story and answer the questions.

Swak! The flyswatter hit the table for another near miss. A fly buzzed tauntingly just above Jeffrey's head. It relaxed and landed on the edge of the window. *Smik!* Julia tallied her 10th kill in a row. "Absolutely no way!" yelled Jeffrey. "There is no way that you can hit those flies every time!"

"It's a good thing for you that I can," said Julia. "You left the sliding door open and let all of those flies come into the house. You know that Mom will have a fit if they're still in here at dinnertime." *Smack!* Julia landed another one as if to prove her point.

Swak! Swak! Swak! Jeffrey missed three more, the sweat running down his face as much from effort as from the heat. "OK, I give up. How do you do it? Last week, you couldn't hit a fly if it was the size of a bird. This week, you can't miss."

"It's knowledge, you know," Julia said. "I checked out a book from the library and found out something interesting about flies—they take off backward."

"What?"

"When a fly takes off, it goes backward and then shoots forward. If you aim right behind their little behinds, you hit them every time."

Jeffrey grinned as he eyed his latest prey.

---

1. What is the setting? _____

2. What is making the sounds *swak*, *smik*, and *smack*? _____

3. What event caused the flies to be in the house? _____

4. Why is Julia able to hit the flies and Jeffrey isn't? _____

5. Who said, "What?" and how can you tell? _____

   _____

6. What do you predict Jeffrey will do next? Highlight the relevant details in the story.

   _____

What Is It?

Read the information on **the ring-tailed lemur card**. Imagine that you are watching a film about animals. Determine whether each animal described could be a ring-tailed lemur. Write **Y** for **yes** or **N** for **no** on the line. If your answer is no, highlight the words that **explain why.**

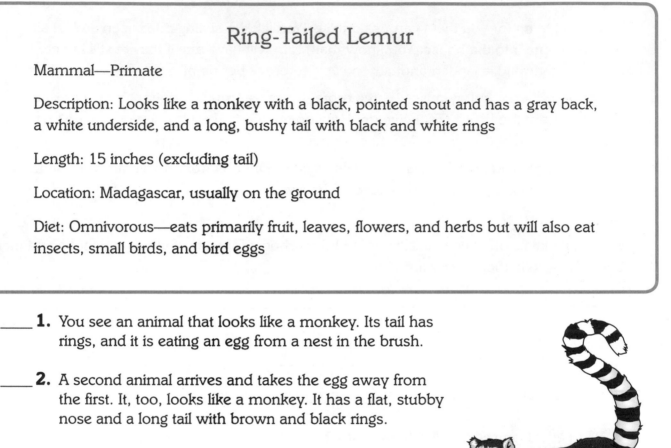

Ring-Tailed Lemur

Mammal—Primate

Description: Looks like a monkey with a black, pointed snout and has a gray back, a white underside, and a long, bushy tail with black and white rings

Length: 15 inches (excluding tail)

Location: Madagascar, usually on the ground

Diet: Omnivorous—eats primarily fruit, leaves, flowers, and herbs but will also eat insects, small birds, and bird eggs

_____ **1.** You see an animal that looks like a monkey. Its tail has rings, and it is eating an egg from a nest in the brush.

_____ **2.** A second animal arrives and takes the egg away from the first. It, too, looks like a monkey. It has a flat, stubby nose and a long tail with brown and black rings.

_____ **3.** A hairy, gray animal is eating fruit and leaves in a tree.

_____ **4.** Emerging from behind a termite mound is a three-foot-long animal with a gray back and white underside.

_____ **5.** A short-tailed animal with a black, pointed snout is lapping up ants. Its four short legs have black and white rings.

_____ **6.** An animal with black and white rings on its tail is sunning itself on the ground.

_____ **7.** The carnivorous gray-and-white mammal is slowly stalking a bird in its nest.

Waiting

Read the passage. Use the information to answer the questions.

Audrey stands alone outside by the side of the road, stamping her feet. The sky begins to turn slate gray. There are no extra colors, not even a minute spark of light. She looks longingly at her home. The lit windows smile warmly at her. Audrey rubs her hands together and blows on their bluing tips. "I should have grabbed my mittens," she thinks. A heavy weight rests in the middle of her back: knowledge.

Shivering neighbors slide quietly into a circle of warmth. Too sleepy to talk, they share body warmth and protection from the wind. Barren trees stand guard as they wait. A pair of wide-spaced lights approaches. The circle stirs. It is a false alarm.

A few minutes later, another pair of lights shines like a pair of eyes in the dim light. A welcoming yellow haven stops and opens, admitting the chilly youngsters into humming warmth. It moves along its ebony ribbon between the trees to other cold huddlers and a final destination that will open their minds.

1. What time of day is it? _____

   Highlight details in the passage that support your answer.

2. Why is Audrey standing by the road? _____

   Highlight details in the passage that support your answer.

3. Which two words best describe Audrey?

   A. cold and tired   **B.** wise and warm   **C.** tired and hungry   **D.** fearful and alert

4. Who are the shivering neighbors? _____

5. What made the circle stir the first time? _____

6. What things do the following phrases describe?

   A. "yellow haven" _____

   B. "destination that will open their minds" _____

   C. "ebony ribbon" _____

   D. "heavy weight . . . in the middle of her back" _____

As you read the study guide below, think of examples of the different states of matter.

- Matter takes up space and has mass.

- There are three states of matter: solid, liquid, and gas.
    solid: is certain size and shape; takes up space; has mass
    liquid: is certain size; takes shape of container; takes up space; has mass
    gas: takes size and shape of container; takes up space; has mass

- Matter has physical properties such as flexibility, color, texture, buoyancy, smell, mass, weight, shape, and size.

- A physical change is a change in shape, size, or state but NOT in type of matter.

- Examples of physical changes to water:
    divide water into two or more containers
    freeze the water (change from liquid to solid)
    melt ice (change from solid to liquid)
    boil water (change from liquid to gas)
    condensation (change from gas to liquid)
    add a substance to it, forming a mixture (examples: adding pepper, rice, etc.)
    crush ice

- A chemical change is a change in type of matter.
  Example: baking a cake

- Two objects cannot occupy the same space at the same time.

- A mixture is a combination of various types of matter in which each maintains its own properties and can be separated out (with tweezers, filter paper, sieve, etc.).
  Example: trail mix

- A solution is a mixture of two or more substances that cannot be separated by mechanical means (with tweezers, filter paper, sieve, etc.).

- Liquid + liquid: become solution, mix together, or separate into levels
  Examples: food coloring in water and column of liquids

- Solid + liquid: sink, float, melt, dissolve, float, or become soggy

- Determine mass based on the position of a pan on a pan balance or a ruler on a ruler balance.
  Example: The apple has more mass because its pan is lower.

- Give evidence that an item has volume. When placing an item in water, the water will rise. The difference in water volume can be measured to determine the item's volume.

Matter

Use the information on the study guide (page 64) to help you answer the following questions.

1. What two characteristics do all states of matter share?

    _____   _____

2. Based on the information given, which state of matter are the following materials?

    pepper _____   air _____

    apple cider _____   chocolate chip _____

    water vapor _____   milk _____

3. Give one more example of each state of matter.

    solid: _____   liquid: _____

    gas: _____

4. What principle of matter does the following passage demonstrate?

    Two students, coming from opposite directions, run around a corner and crash into each other. Both end up staggering backward.

    _____

    _____

5. Based on the information given, write three physical properties of this paper.

    _____   _____   _____

6. List two ways that you could cause a physical change to occur to this paper.

    _____   _____

7. Are you made of matter? Give evidence to support your answer. _____

    _____

    _____

    _____

8. You have a bowl of trail mix. It contains pretzels, raisins, peanuts, oat cereal, and chocolate chips. Is it a mixture or a solution? _____

Ladybug Letter

Read the letter.

Dear Jeremy,

Remember when we learned how good ladybugs are for plants last year? We found out that they eat harmful insects, like aphids and the cottony-cushion scale. Some gardeners and farmers even pay to have ladybugs shipped to them for plant protection. Just a few of these beetles can eat hundreds of harmful insects from one tree, reducing the need for pesticides.

Well, my mom, who usually loves having the oval, spotted insects around our garden, has a different opinion right now. You'll never believe what happened! Our house has become one huge, ladybug mansion. Mom is going bonkers!

We learned in school that ladybugs love to crawl onto leaves and into cracks in trees. I found out that they crawl into cracks in houses, too! When I came home last Tuesday, the sides of our house and all of the screens were covered with ladybugs. They even came inside the house through the air conditioning unit upstairs. The upstairs ceiling was covered. I found about 70 of the bugs clustered behind a curtain on a window upstairs. My sister is having fun trying to catch them in the bathroom. She has jars filled with the little crawlies.

Mom has been calling gardening stores and searching the Internet. She found out that the beetles are attracted to light-colored buildings, especially those warmed by the sun. Boy, is she rethinking that decision to paint the house white! Once they get inside, it's hard to get rid of ladybugs. If you disturb them, they secrete a nasty-smelling, yellow liquid from their leg joints. Vacuuming them is one solution. People should also check the siding and window openings and caulk any cracks around dryer vents and windows. Mom has Dad recaulking any windows that look like they have openings big enough for those little buggers.

I managed to get extra credit in my science and math classes from this! I did some research for my science report. I learned that the two-spotted ladybug is the most common. I decided to count the spots on some of our ladybugs. Of the 256 critters I looked at, fewer than 30 had one or two spots. In fact, 197 of them had more than six spots. I looked on the Internet and found out why. Here in the northern United States, ladybugs have more spots because the darker spots help them retain more heat. That sure explained what was going on at my house.

I hope you have just dust bunnies, dirt, and some cookie crumbs to vacuum at your house. If you need an extra credit project, just stop over. See you soon.

Your friend,

Ian

Ladybug Letter

Use the letter to answer the following questions.

1. What other words does Ian use in place of the word *ladybugs* in his letter?
   List six of them.

   _____   _____   _____

   _____   _____   _____

2. Why do you think the ladybugs chose Ian's house? Give two reasons. _____

   _____

   _____

   Highlight with green key words and phrases in the text that support your answer.

3. What are two ways to get rid of unwanted ladybugs?

   _____   _____

4. How are ladybugs useful? _____

5. When do ladybugs become a nuisance? _____

   _____

   Highlight with yellow key words and phrases in the text that support your answer.

6. How does Ian's mother feel about ladybugs? _____

   _____

   Explain your answer. _____

   _____

   _____

7. Why did the majority of Ian's ladybugs have more than six spots? _____

   _____

8. Where in the house did Ian and his family find ladybugs? Highlight four locations in the
   text with yellow.

Three Levels of Questions

Read the questions. Evaluate how you would answer each one. Write the level of the question on the line using the key.

> Level 1 = yes or no responses
> Level 2 = one-word or short answer
> Level 3 = extended answer

_____ 1. Where is the Grand Canyon?

_____ 2. How do you make chocolate chip cookies?

_____ 3. Do people float in space?

_____ 4. Why is a launch tube needed?

_____ 5. What is the name of the winning football team?

_____ 6. What is the source of the light?

_____ 7. When do monarch butterflies migrate?

_____ 8. Why is diabetes a problem for some people?

_____ 9. When is soccer season?

_____ 10. How does a virus invade the body?

_____ 11. Will it take two weeks to grow?

_____ 12. Where do anemones live?

_____ 13. What part of a submarine makes it float?

_____ 14. How do I apply for a position with the school paper?

_____ 15. How is energy delivered from the dam to houses?

_____ 16. How does a spider make a web?

_____ 17. Do cheetahs run faster than elephants?

_____ 18. Will you study for the test with me?

A. Highlight the first word in each question.
1 = yellow   2 = green   3 = red

B. Which level of question do you think leads to the best group discussions? Why? _____

_____

C. List the beginning words for each level of question in the chart below. Using information from the chart, can you draw any conclusions about the three levels of questions? Write your conclusions on a separate sheet of paper.

Level 1	Level 2	Level 3

Camping on Frog Pond

author's viewpoint and word choices

Read the two campers' descriptions of waking up at Frog Pond. Then, answer the following questions.

Camper One

We woke this morning to waves lapping the shore, a breeze rustling the leaves, and baby frogs croaking to each other. They woke the swans and ducks, who sang good morning to the animals around the pond. Soon, every insect, bird, and animal was calling good morning to each other. How could I stay in bed? I needed to greet the morning, too.

Camper Two

We woke this morning to the incessant sound of frogs in the pond. Their noisy alarm triggered off-key honking and quacking from around the pond. The waves slapped the shore while the wind sandpapered everything in its path. Within 60 seconds, every insect, bird, and animal seemed to be protesting the hour. With this continuous cacophony, it was hardly worth going back to sleep.

1. How does Camper One feel about waking up at Frog Pond? _____

_____

Highlight words in the description that support your answer.

2. How does Camper Two feel about waking up at Frog Pond? _____

_____

Highlight words in the description that support your answer.

3. After reading both pieces, write four facts about what happened at Frog Pond that morning. Do not include any opinion words.

_____

_____

_____

_____

4. Imagine that you went camping at Frog Pond. Write a description of your trip. Use words that will show readers whether you enjoyed your camping trip.

_____

_____

_____

_____

Summer Bridge Reading RB-904096

Check Your Summary

A **summary** provides a snapshot of a passage. It should include only details that support the main idea.

Read the summaries. Circle the main idea of each summary. Then, underline the detail that does not support the main idea.

1. Household measuring tools are found in a variety of places. Thermometers are found in water heaters, ovens, and microwaves. Carpets help keep your feet warm. Measuring cups and spoons are in nearly every kitchen. Clocks can be found in bedrooms, kitchens, and bathrooms.

2. Rain forest plants are the topic of the article that I read. Rain forests have animals, like monkeys and sloths. Numerous flowering plants and vines grow on the forest floor. Many of the trees grow to the heights of city buildings. Bromeliads are plants that grow in the canopy of the rain forest.

3. Computers have many uses. They are used to access the Internet. Their word processing programs are used for reports, letters, and schoolwork. They are also used for recreational and educational computer games. Computers even come in many different colors.

4. People believe in many different superstitions. Some people are fearful of numbers, like 13. Others believe in lucky tokens like rabbits' feet. Many people think that superstitions are silly. Some people are certain that you will have seven years of bad luck if you break a mirror.

5. People react differently to anesthesia. Crying uncontrollably is one reaction. Some people become sleepy for several hours after surgery. Anesthesia makes surgery easy for people because they don't experience any pain. Another reaction is becoming temperamental.

6. Limited television-viewing time is important for students and families. It helps students learn by providing more study time. Watching educational television is better than watching horror shows. Less television viewing allows children to have more time to exercise and play. It also gives families more time to interact.

Summary Focus

A **summary focus statement** is a single sentence that describes the topic of a story.

Read the textual details for each summary. Then, circle the best summary focus statement.

1. First, it costs almost a cent to make a cent. Counting and adding pennies takes up a lot of time. Many people do not like having pennies take up space in their pockets, wallets, and purses.

   A. This article tells that the government makes about 14 billion pennies each year.

   B. This article explains many reasons why people think that cents do not make sense.

   C. This article outlines the history of the penny.

2. Banff National Park is located in Alberta, Canada. It is Canada's oldest national park. Quebec, Canada, is home to the Mingan Archipelago National Park Reserve. The archipelago is made up of 40 limestone islands and more than 1,000 granite reefs and islets. Kluane National Park and Reserve in Yukon, Canada, is home to Mount Logan, Canada's highest peak.

   A. The brochure describes and gives the locations of many Canadian national parks.

   B. The brochure describes Canada's historic sites.

   C. The brochure describes Canada's 10 provinces and 3 territories.

3. Salvador Dalí was a famous Spanish artist. He was born in 1904 and lived until 1989. Dalí, one of the greatest artists of the 20th century, was a surrealist painter who found fantasy to be an inspiration.

   A. This book is about surrealist painters.

   B. This anthology of biographies is about painters of the 1900s.

   C. This biography is about Salvador Dalí.

4. Its blubber acts as an insulating layer. The blowhole acts as the whale's nose. The melon is the bulging forehead that cushions the beluga as it forces its way through the ice.

   A. This Web site explains the life cycle of the beluga whale.

   B. This Web site explains the functions of the beluga whale's different body parts.

   C. This Web site discusses the beluga whale's eating habits.

Each person in Aziza's class was assigned to interview a professional and write a summary of the interview. Aziza interviewed her optometrist, Dr. Iris. Read Aziza's interview with Dr. Iris and answer the following questions.

Aziza: I am interested in finding out how to care for my eyes when they have problems. What should I do if I get something in my eye? Rub it?

Dr. Iris: Never rub your eye if there is something in it. You could scratch your cornea. Pull your upper lashes out gently to lift your upper eyelid. Pull it very gently over your lower eyelashes. This can cause the object to fall out or your eyes to tear and wash out the object.

Aziza: What if that doesn't work?

Dr. Iris: Then, seek medical attention right away.

Aziza: What if a chemical gets into my eye?

Dr. Iris: Immediately flush your eyes with warm water, preferably from a faucet but you may also use a cup. Do this for at least 20 minutes. See a doctor or call the poison control center.

Aziza: What should I do for a black eye?

Dr. Iris: Get a cool, wet washcloth. Press it gently on the eye for about 15 minutes every hour. It is a good idea to have a doctor check the eye for internal damage.

Aziza: OK, here's a gross one: what should I do if something cuts my eye or gets stuck in my eye?

Dr. Iris: The "getting stuck" is called penetration. If either of these things happen, *Do not* flush your eye, try to take out the object, or put any medicine on it. Gently cover the eye with gauze or a bandage and go straight to the nearest emergency room.

Aziza: Thank you, Dr. Iris. I learned a lot about caring for my eyes.

Dr. Iris: You're welcome, Aziza. It is important to take good care of your eyes. You get only one pair. Be sure to have your eyes checked once a year.

1.   Help Aziza with her summary. List four things that Dr. Iris told her that she could do when her eyes had a problem. Highlight words and phrases in the text that support your answer.

_____   _____

_____   _____

2.   What would be the best topic sentence for Aziza's interview summary?

   A. It is important to know what to do when your eyes have a problem.

   B. See your eye doctor once a year.

   C. You get only one pair of eyes.

   D. Gross things can happen to your eyes.

Bamboo

Read the passage.

When bamboo comes to mind, so do images of pandas and China. While this plant is well known for its role in the life cycle of China's endangered pandas, it is now becoming known for its own deterioration. Deforestation is threatening the habitats of as many as half of the world's species of bamboo.

Bamboo has many interesting characteristics. Bamboo is a woody plant, but it is not a tree. It belongs to the grass family. It is the fastest-growing plant on this planet. One species can grow up to four feet in 24 hours. It grows more than 30% faster than the fastest-growing tree. There are more than 1,200 species of bamboo. They are divided by their rhizome, or root, structures into two main types. Sympodial bamboos have clumps of roots and are commonly called "clumpers"; monopodial bamboos have roots that are runners and are commonly called "runners." Clumpers tend to grow in tropical climates, while runners grow in temperate climates.

These fast-growing plants share a unique characteristic: they rarely bloom. Each species blooms only once every 7 to 120 years, not every year like most plants. Most bamboo of the same species bloom at approximately the same time. Usually, the parent plant dies soon after flowering.

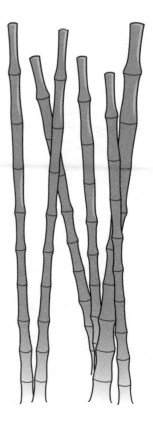

Bamboo is delicate when it emerges from the ground, but it soon becomes one of the most hardy plants around. The plant craves water when it is first planted, but within a year, it can be somewhat drought tolerant. It tolerates precipitation extremes from 30 to 250 inches of rainfall per year. One grove of bamboo even withstood the atomic blast at Hiroshima and within days sent up new shoots. It was the first regreening in that devastated area.

Bamboo has many uses. It grows fast, with some types reaching a mature height in just two months. India, China, and Burma have found that a grove of bamboo can be harvested and make a profit in as little as 3 to 5 years. This is much better than rattan, which takes 8 to 10 years to make a profit, and most softwoods, which are generally grown in the United States and Canada and cannot be harvested for 10 to 20 years.

Bamboo is an excellent building material. It is pliable and one of the strongest building materials. In fact, its tensile strength is greater than steel's. Tensile strength refers to how well a material resists breaking under pressure. Steel has a tensile strength of 23,000 psi, while bamboo's tensile strength is a superior 28,000 psi. Bamboo is also an excellent structural material for buildings in earthquake-prone areas. In fact, after the violent 1992 earthquake in Limón, Costa Rica, only the National Bamboo Project's bamboo houses were left standing.

Bamboo (continued)

The history of electric lights started with bamboo. Thomas Edison used bamboo during his first experiment with the lightbulb. He used a piece of carbonized bamboo for the filament, or the part that glows to make light. It worked, and light was produced.

Soil conservation is another use of bamboo. Because it grows and matures quickly, it can be planted in deforested areas that have trouble with erosion. Its dense root systems hold the soil in place. Bamboo can also be used to strengthen areas of land that are prone to mud slides and earthquakes.

Bamboo is used to make many items that we use daily. Bamboo pulp is used to make paper. It is also used to make paneling, floor tiles, briquettes for fuel, and rebar to reinforce concrete beams. An antioxidant in pulverized bamboo bark helps prevent the growth of bacteria and is commonly used as a natural food preservative, especially in Japan.

Pandas need bamboo; it may be essential to their survival. Bamboo needs each of us. When we learn to use it to its full potential, we will no longer have to watch it deteriorate or fear that it will become endangered.

Write a summary of the passage. Continue on another sheet of paper, if necessary. Craft your summary statement so that each detail sentence fits the focus.

_____

_____

_____

_____

_____

_____

_____

_____

Sunset

Read the poem in the box. Then, complete the activities.

> **Sunset**
>
> Blaze extinguished
>
> Smoldering
>
> Blanket of ash
>
> Speckled with fireflies

1. To what does this poem compare a sunset? _____

2. Draw a line from each line of the poem to its literal interpretation.

Blaze extinguished   the sky graying at dusk

Smoldering   the stars sparkling across the sky

Blanket of ash   the sun going below the horizon

Speckled with fireflies   the shades of pink, red, purple, and
                                            orange expanding above the horizon

3. Draw the sequence of events described in the poem.

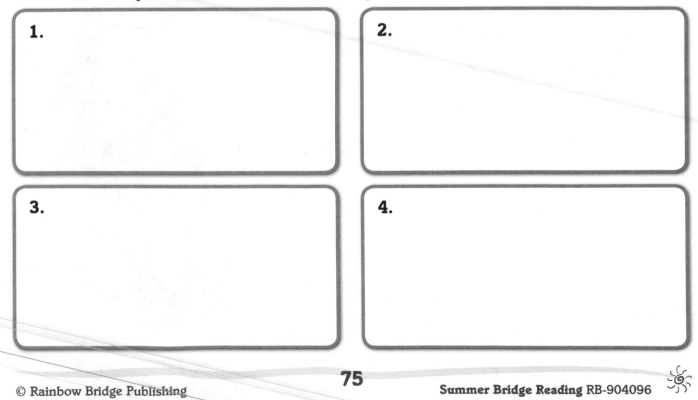

1.

2.

3.

4.

Summer Bridge Reading RB-904096

Mountain Reminiscence

As I sat exhausted on the trail,
I noticed a squirrel with a big, fluffy tail.
The very sight of him made me smile,
For I knew he'd be my friend all the while.

When I watched my little friend work,
I stood up with a sudden jerk.
My friend had inspired me; indeed he had.
He'd shown me that it wasn't so bad.

I'd become tired and had stopped to rest,
But the squirrel was so tireless; he passed the test!
He reminded me to never quit;
Just keep on going and always remember it!

So, I started to climb again with a new surge of strength
As I followed the trail up the mountain's length.
I later grew tired again as I climbed,
But I did not stop and I did not look behind.

I had to make it; I knew that I could,
And I knew that I would.
Then, at last, I reached the top,
And not until then, did I let myself stop.

When I took a look around,
I could hardly believe what I had found.
It was the most wonderful sight I had ever seen,
And then, I felt as glorious as a queen.

I had not stopped, and now I was glad,
For if I had, I would have later been mad.
But, I was especially thankful for my squirrel friend,
Who had taught me to push until the very end!

Mountain Reminiscence

After reading "Mountain Reminiscence," (page 76) answer the following questions.

1. The main idea of the poem "Mountain Reminiscence" is

    A. that it is fun to hike in the mountains.

    B. that you should never give up when you are working toward a goal.

    C. that it is not fun to have animals as friends.

    D. that you should be careful when you are climbing in the woods.

2. What is the term for words, like *trail* and *tail*, that sound alike at the end of poetic lines (see lines 1 and 2 in the poem)?

    A. simile   **B.** alliteration   **C.** metaphor   **D.** rhyme

3. The word *reminiscence* in the title means

    A. retreat.   **B.** adventure.   **C.** remember.   **D.** friend.

4. "I felt as glorious as a queen." What form of figurative language is used in this line of poetry?

    A. simile   **B.** personification   **C.** metaphor   **D.** pun

5. Which of the following words is an antonym for *tireless*?

    A. energetic   **B.** tired   **C.** unending   **D.** stimulating

6. The squirrel in this poem is being personified as a/an/the

    A. mountain.   **B.** enemy.   **C.** woods.   **D.** friend.

7. The setting for this poem is a/an

    A. valley.   **B.** ocean.   **C.** mountain.   **D.** cabin.

8. "My friend had *inspired* me; indeed he had." Choose a word that has the same meaning as the italicized word.

    A. encouraged   **B.** trusted   **C.** insulted   **D.** disheartened

Summer Bridge Reading RB-904096

Poetry Terms

Use the following clues to complete the crossword puzzle (page 79).

Across

3.   a comparison between two unlike things

7.   the formal rhythm of a poem, often used with rhyme

9.   A simile uses the word _____ or *as*.

10. an implied comparison between an object and a human being

11. a comparison using the word *like* or *as*

Down

1.   a group of words that start with the same sound

2.   a word or phrase that sounds like what it describes

4.   at least two words that end with the same sound

5.   a repeated vowel sound

6.   Alliterative words begin with the _____ sound.

8.   the beat of a poem

> rhythm
>
> meter
>
> alliteration
>
> simile
>
> rhyme
>
> metaphor
>
> onomatopoeia
>
> like
>
> assonance
>
> same
>
> personification

Extra! Write an original example of each poetic device.

1.   alliteration _____

2.   onomatopoeia _____

3.   simile _____

4.   metaphor _____

5.   rhyme _____

Summer Bridge Reading RB-904096

Poetry Terms

Complete the crossword puzzle using the clues (page 78).

Read the poem in the box. Then, answer the following questions.

> **Winter Sunrise**
>
> Rose fingernails push back
> star-sparkled blanket.
> Warm toes slide out,
> feel cold morning.
> Pink pajama-clad body sits on side of bed,
> shivering,
> standing,
> stretching.
> Sparkle . . .
> A snow day.

1. To what does this poem compare a sunrise? _____

2. Think of a sunrise. Make connections between the poem and an actual sunrise. Write a

literal interpretation for each image.

Fingernails: _____

Blanket: _____

Toes: _____

Body: _____

3. Draw a picture in the box to illustrate the sunrise in the poem.

Guide Words

> **Guide words** help you locate entries in a dictionary. Guide words are a pair of words that are printed at the top of each page in a dictionary. They are determined by alphabetical order. The first guide word is alphabetically the first word on the page. The second guide word is the last entry on the page.

Circle your answers.

1. The guide words are *justice* and *juvenile*. Locate the word *just*.

   A. previous page   **B.** this page   **C.** next page

2. The guide words are *wont* and *woodsy*. Which word is not on the page?

   A. wood   **B.** wonder   **C.** woodchuck

3. Look at the guide words. On what page will you find the word *fugal*?

   A. fry—fuel   **B.** fug—fuji   **C.** full—fumble

4. The guide words are *yearbook* and *yellow jacket*. Which word is on the page?

   A. yellow   **B.** year   **C.** yelp

5. Which word will be last on the page?

   A. payable   **B.** payee   **C.** pay

6. Which word will be first on the page?

   A. halfpenny   **B.** half   **C.** halfway

7. The guide words are *sealant* and *seatrain*. Which word is not on the page?

   A. seat   **B.** seal   **C.** search

8. The guide words are *applejack* and *apply*. Which word is on the page?

   A. appreciate   **B.** application   **C.** apple

9. The guide words are *bloom* and *blouse*. Locate the word *blot*.

   A. previous page   **B.** this page   **C.** next page

10. Look at the guide words. On what page will you find the word *long*?

    A. longevous—look   **B.** look—loony   **C.** lonesome—longitude

Library Work

Find an example of each reference resource listed below. Check the box when you locate each one. Write a description or definition of the resource on the line.

☐ atlas: _____

☐ dictionary: _____

☐ encyclopedia: _____

☐ glossary: _____

☐ index: _____

☐ thesaurus: _____

Write the best resource for the task on each line.

1. Locate the pronunciation of *scrivener* or *scudo*. _____

2. Find a different word for *excellent* since you have used it six times in your paper.

_____

3. Determine the continent(s) that border Asia. _____

4. Find more than 15 definitions for *run*. _____

5. Find the definition of *scalene* in your math book. _____

6. Locate the pages in your science book that refer to plant roots. _____

7. Gather information about castles for your class report. _____

8. The word *genealogy* is in bold print in your social studies book, and you want to know what it means. _____

9. Get the information needed to label the countries of South America on your map.

_____

10. Find seven facts about roller coasters. _____

Navigating the Library's Research Section   using reference resources

Circle the letter next to the answer to each question.

1. In which reference work would you find the best maps of countries mentioned in the book *Domino Effect*?

    A. dictionary

    B. atlas

    C. thesaurus

2. In which reference work would you find the best definition of the word *congregate*?

    A. dictionary

    B. atlas

    C. encyclopedia

3. In which reference work would you find information about the history and economy of Honduras?

    A. dictionary

    B. thesaurus

    C. encyclopedia

4. Guide words are in _____ order.

    A. numerical

    B. cylindrical

    C. alphabetical

5. In an encyclopedia, the entry for China would be between which two entries?

    A. flower and France

    B. Singapore and Spain

    C. cat and chocolate

6. In a dictionary, the entry for the word *meticulous* would be on the same page with which two guide words?

    A. metaphor and metric

    B. malign and mammal

    C. monochrome and monument

7. In which reference resource would you find the capital of Holland?

    A. thesaurus

    B. atlas

    C. dictionary

8. Where would you find information about the life and works of William Wordsworth?

    A. dictionary

    B. encyclopedia

    C. atlas

© Rainbow Bridge Publishing   Summer Bridge Reading RB-904096

Parts of a Book

Read the choices in the box. Write the correct choice on each line.

> ### Parts of a Book
>
> | Copyright Page | Index | Appendix |
> | Table of Contents | Acknowledgements | Bibliography |

1. Which part of a book comes after the text and gives additional information?

   _____

2. Which part of a book comes before the text and shows how the book is organized?

   _____

3. Which part of a book comes after the text and lists subjects in alphabetical order?

   _____

4. Which part of a book comes after the text and lists books that the author consulted?

   _____

5. Which part of a book comes before the text and gives credit to people who helped the author?

   _____

6. Which part of a book comes before the text and gives the copyright date?

   _____

> **Extra!** Examine a history or science textbook. Locate the parts of the book. Find as many of the book parts as you can. Why does a book need both a table of contents and an index?_____
>
> _____
>
> _____

Read the passage.

Your brain is constantly making pathways and interconnecting experiences. This allows you to access vivid mental images, emotions, and even smells when you hear about, read about, or think about certain events. When you think of the word *father* or *mother*, a mental image immediately comes to mind. An emotion may also register, especially if your father just did something nice for you. Think about the word *pond*. Each person sees a mental picture based on his own experience. Does your image have a white, sandy beach, or is grass growing down to the water's edge? Is the water clear and blue, or is the surface covered with lily pads and duckweed?

Your understanding is influenced by the previous knowledge that you have tucked away into mental file cabinets. Being aware of the connecting experiences increases your understanding of new experiences. This is especially true when it comes to understanding what you read; all of your past knowledge impacts what you comprehend.

Your past knowledge can come from personal experience, things you have seen in electronic format, books, or information someone else has
shared with you. Each time a tie, or reference, is made between bits of mental information, it provides additional routes for retrieving it again from the billions of thoughts that have been placed into your mental haystacks. For example, while Meg was reading two different books about boys living in the wilderness, she thought about times that she had spent in woodland environments camping with her family, hiking with friends, and canoeing. She thought about mosquitoes and poison ivy, but she also thought about how clear the sky was at night and about the forest animals she had seen. Meg also remembered a newscast about deforestation, as well as numerous books about the outdoors that she had read over the years. Each connection helped Meg become more involved in each book and increased her understanding and enjoyment of the two books.

1. Highlight with green four specific details about mental connections or touch points in the passage.

2. Highlight with yellow the four places from which the past knowledge for mental connections can come.

Touch Points

Read the entries Meg made in her Mental Connections chart. Use the information from her chart to complete the activity.

Event in Story	Mental Connection
Pete, the boy in the story, talks about being hungry. He finds a berry patch and picks some berries to eat. Pete talks about how tasty they are. Later, however, he gets a stomachache from eating only berries.	This reminds me of my family. Every summer, we pick strawberries, raspberries, and blueberries. I know how long it can take to pick them and how delicious they are when you are hungry. Getting a stomachache from eating too many berries on an empty stomach is also a familiar feeling for me.
Pete needs to find shelter. He looks around, but there isn't much to be found in the wilderness. He becomes panicky; he isn't prepared to live in the wild. He finally finds a cave-like opening that he can make into a place to sleep.	This reminds me of the last book I read. In that book, a boy named Neil also needs to find shelter. The difference is that he had done some research on living in the wild. I'll bet that Pete would appreciate some of Neil's books.
Pete is found. He is glad to be going home. He is also very proud that he was able to survive on his own for three months.	Learning from a difficult situation . . . _____ _____ _____

1. Read the first entry. List two specific parallel connections.

    text: _____   text: _____

    Meg: _____   Meg: _____

2. To what did Meg connect the first event? Circle your answer.

    A. another text   **B.** a personal experience

    C. a news incident   **D.** a TV program

3. What connections does Meg make between the book she is reading now and the last book that she read? _____

    _____

4. Complete the last entry in the chart under Mental Connection with your own mental connection.

Opinion Papers

Iesha and her classmates each wrote an opinion paper on the sun. They were required to refer to information studied about the sun and take a position on whether the sun is good, and defend that position. Iesha and Jackie made a Venn diagram based on their papers. Use the information from the diagram below to answer the questions (page 88).

causes sunburn

gives people jobs

melts ice

tans people's skin

causes floods by melting ice and snow

is a star

causes aurora borealis

causes skin cancer through overexposure

is the center of our solar system (Earth revolves around it.)

provides warmth for enjoying the beach

makes it too hot in summer

is a clean energy source (solar energy)

makes it too hot and dry in deserts

ejects solar winds

activates plant chlorophyll

is not in many places enough to make solar energy worthwhile

affects weather

dries up mud

dries out lawns and gardens

usage of fossil fuels

makes people happy

inspires people to eat ice cream

causes damage during droughts

inspires artists

Iesha

Jackie

Opinion Papers

Read the following statements. Whose paper is more likely to contain each one? Write *Iesha*, *Jackie*, or *both* on the line next to the statement.

_____ **1.** The sun withers millions of acres of farmland each year.

_____ **2.** Although solar energy may help those in sunny climates, those who live in the north find it worthless. Some communities see the sun fewer than three months each year.

_____ **3.** If there were no sun, going to the beach would not be fun. This star at the center of our solar system provides the warmth needed for this excursion.

_____ **4.** The sun has inspired artists throughout the ages. Any art museum provides proof.

_____ **5.** The aurora borealis, or northern lights, is an incredible display of waving colors thanks to solar winds.

_____ **6.** This joy-inspiring star provides a guide for its revolving planets.

_____ **7.** The planets that revolve around the sun burn or freeze depending on how far they are away from it. The only one in exactly the right position to sustain human life is Earth.

_____ **8.** The sun has devastated many areas when it melts snow and ice, causing flooding.

Choose a topic from each student's part of the Venn diagram. Highlight the topics. Then, write a sentence or two about the topic using the voice and opinion of that student.

Iesha: _____

_____

_____

_____

Jackie: _____

_____

_____

_____

African American Time Line

Use the time line to answer the questions (page 90).

1837 — James McCune Smith is the first African American to earn a medical degree.

1847 — Frederick Augustus Douglass buys his freedom and becomes a newspaper publisher.

1870 — Joseph H. Rainey of South Carolina is the first African American to serve in the U.S. House of Representatives.

1878 — Joseph Winters invents the fire-escape ladder.

1881 — Booker T. Washington founds Tuskegee Institute.

1882 — Benjamin "Pap" Singleton is given a Grand Complimentary Anniversary Celebration.

1882 — Lewis Latimer patents the carbon lightbulb filament.

1890 — William Purvis patents a fountain pen that has its own ink.

1091 — Phillip Downing designs and patents the big, blue, street-corner mailbox.

1897 — Henry O. Tanner's painting *Resurrection of Lazarus* is declared a masterpiece and purchased by the French government.

1899 — George Grant patents a wooden golf tee.

1909 — Matthew Henson reaches the North Pole on April 6.

1913 — Harriet Tubman is buried in New York with military honors.

1923 — Garrett Morgan invents the automatic traffic light.

1950 — Gwendolyn Brooks is the first African American to be awarded a Pulitzer Prize.

1963 — Dr. Martin Luther King Jr. leads the peace march in Washington, D.C., and makes his famous "I have a dream" speech.

1967 — Thurgood Marshall is the first African American associate justice of the Supreme Court.

1968 — Shirley Chisholm is the first African American woman elected to Congress.

1976 — Alex Haley publishes *Roots: The Saga of an American Family*.

1983 — Guion S. Bluford Jr. goes into space aboard the space shuttle *Challenger*.

African American Time Line

Use the time line (page 89) to answer the following questions.

1. In what year was Gwendolyn Brooks awarded the Pulitzer Prize? _____

2. Alex Haley's *Roots* was made into a television miniseries in 1977. How many years was his book in print before the miniseries was made? _____

3. What year would you have been able to use a pen with its own ink instead of carrying an ink bottle? _____

4. This woman, who died in 1913, led more than 300 slaves to freedom. At one time, a reward of $40,000—quite a lot of money at the time—was offered to anyone who could capture her. Who was she? _____

5. In what year did Joseph Winters invent the fire escape ladder? _____

6. Pap Singleton founded Singleton Colony, a place for former slaves to settle, in Kansas. In what year was a celebration held in his honor? _____

7. Which happened first: an African American entered the House of Representatives or the Supreme Court?

   _____

8. What leading African American spokesman bought his freedom in 1847? _____

   _____

9. The first hospital for African Americans was opened in 1833 in Savannah, Georgia. Would Dr. McCune Smith have been able to practice there during the year that it opened? Why or why not?

   _____

   _____

10. Which inventor worked with Thomas Edison and made the carbon lightbulb filament?

   _____

Bicycle Safety

Fiona presented a report on bicycle safety to her class. She polled her classmates about their own bicycle safety before and after her presentation. She then compiled the information into the following table.

Question	Safety before Report		Safety after Report	
	Yes	No	Yes	No
Do you think that you will always check your brakes, seat, handlebars, and tires before riding your bike?	1	24	16	9
Do you think that you will always wear a helmet?	9	16	22	3
Do you think that you will always pay attention to all traffic signs?	12	13	22	3
Do you think that you will regularly ride on the handlebars or with two people on a bike?	10	15	2	23
Do you think that you will always walk your bike across busy intersections?	3	22	22	3

Use the information in the tables above to answer the following questions.

1. Compare the sets of data from before and after Fiona's report. Write two true, specific statements comparing them here.

   _____

   _____

2. Which of the following statements about the class is true before Fiona's report?

   A. The class has no bicycle safety habits.

   B. The class's bicycle safety needs some improvement.

   C. The class is already good at bicycle safety.

3. Which of the following statements is true after Fiona's report?

   A. Everyone will use bicycle safety habits.

   B. Her report has no effect on her classmates' safety habits.

   C. Most of the class is committed to having better bicycle safety habits.

4. Based on the data, what conclusion could Fiona make about her report?

   A. Her report influenced her classmates.

   B. Her report was about safety.

   C. Her report did not get a passing grade.

Sleep Tight

Read the text and look at the table. Then, answer the following questions.

Getting enough sleep is extremely important. During sleep, the heart, lungs, muscles, nervous system, digestive system, and skeletal system rest and get ready for another busy day. Insufficient sleep results in a sleep debt, or an amount of sleep that is owed to your body. Sleep debt definitely affects how a person functions. People with this deficit may not think that they are sleepy, but they are less able to concentrate. They are also irritable and emotional and may have slow reactions. In fact, some people with sleep debts can act in ways that mimic the symptoms of attention deficit disorder (ADD). Uninterrupted sleep in which the sleeper reaches and maintains REM, or rapid eye movement, is the key. In this stage of sleep, the body and brain get the relief needed in order to function at their optimum levels the next day. Every individual has his own sleep needs, but researchers have determined the approximate amount of sleep needed by children. These times do not include time in bed spent reading, talking, or thinking about the next day.

Amount of Sleep Needed by Children

Age	Suggested Hours of Uninterrupted Sleep
1–6 years old	10–12 hours
6–12 years old	9–11 hours
12–18 years old	8–10 hours

1. According to this table, if an 11-year-old wakes up at 6:30 A.M., what is the latest time she should fall asleep? _____

2. What is a sleep debt? _____

_____

3. Why is sleep so important? _____

_____

4. What happens to a person who does not get enough sleep? Name two effects.

_____

_____

5. What type of sleep is the most important for your body? _____

Sleep Tight (continued)

6. According to the table, how much sleep should you get each night?_____

7. What time do you get up in the morning? _____

    What is the latest time you should fall asleep each night? _____

8. If you were to sleep the greatest amount of recommended hours, what time would you fall asleep? _____

9. What time did you go to sleep last night? _____

    According to the table, did you get enough sleep? _____

Use the graph to record the amount of time you sleep over the course of one week. Write the days across the bottom. Begin with yesterday and the number of hours you slept last night.

Weekly Sleep Chart

Hours							
13							
12							
11							
10							
9							
8							
7							
6							
5							
4							
3							
2							
1							

Days of the Week

Evaluate your graph. Write two true statements based upon the data you collected.

_____

_____

_____

Answer Key

Page 9
1. date, B.; 2. city, C.; 3. company, B.; 4. temperature, A.; 5. when, C.; 6. long, B.; 7. where, A.; 8. direction, A.; 9. color, C.; 10. cost, C.; 11. what, B.; 12. ocean, A.

Page 10
1. 28; 2. 125; 3. Main Dishes; 4. 15; 5. Breads and Rolls; 6. Just for Kids; 7. Desserts; 8. Cakes and Pies; 9.–11. Answers will vary.; 12. look at the Recipe Index

Page 11
1. milk, tea, water, soda; 2. vowle; 3. complete, entire; 4. through, blew, tough, enough; 5. China; 6. tarantula; 7. Orion; 8. biography, diorama; 9. wood, ice, paper; 10. pedal

Page 12
Answers will vary.

Page 15
1. Answers will vary but may include forests, deserts, backyard, gardens, tundra, grasslands, prairie, tropics, coast, beach, etc.; 2. B.; 3. A.; 4. A.; 5. B.; 6. A.

Page 16
Posters should have all of the elements from the directions.

Page 17
1. B.; 2. A.; 3. C.; 4. B.; 5. A.; 6. A.

Page 18
1. B.; 2. C.; 3. B.; 4. A.; 5. A.; 6. C.; 7. A.; 8. B.; 9. B.; 10. C.

Page 19
6, 5, 2, 7, 4, 1, 3

Page 20
6, 4, 8, 1, 3, 5, 7, 2

Page 22
1. a bad day; 2. He didn't pick up the penny.; 3. a good day; 4. the penny; 5. Answers will vary.; 8, 6, 3, 2, 7, 1, 5, 4

Page 24
1. Answers will vary.; 2. to grab the reader's attention; 3. Answers will vary.; 4. Answers will vary.; 3, 5, 6, 1, 4, 2

Page 25
1. fact; 2. opinion; 3. opinion; 4. fact;

Page 25 (continued)
5. opinion; 6. opinion; 7. fact; 8. opinion; 9. opinion; 10. opinion; 11. fact; 12. opinion; 13.–14. Answers will vary.

Page 26
1. O; 2. F; 3. O; 4. F; 5. F; 6. F; 7. O; 8. F; 9. F; 10. O; 11. F; 12. O; 13. O; 14. F; A.–B. Answers will vary.

Page 27
1. Answers will vary but may include neat, eerie, stringy-looking, disgusting, nasty, gross, slimy, worse, gruesome, repulsive, horrible; 2. Answers will vary.

Page 28
1. R; 2. F; 3. F; 4. R; 5. R; 6. F; 7. R; 8. R; 9. F; 10. F; 11.–12. Answers will vary.

Page 30
1. The kids play a game of freeze-tag-style kick the can.; 2. When the kids are tagged, they have to stop and stand as though they are frozen.; 3. Frizorio cheats by picking up the can and putting it in his pocket.; 4. Miguel doesn't want his sister to play and is trying to scare her.; 5. Frizorio is the name that they give to the person who is "it."; 6. The can is a soda can or an old soup can.; 7. Frizorio is running across the yard when Miguel reaches the can.; 8. Frizorio's sister is tired of his cheating; she catches him and makes him stop.; 9. Westy is an older sister who thinks that the game is for kids.; 10. Miguel runs as fast as he can.

Page 31
1. Juan pushes the swing.; 2. Tien continues in a back and forward arc.; 3. She bumps the bag.; 4. It explodes.; 5. She wants a puppy.; 6. Her parents are impressed and let her get a puppy.; 7.–8. Answers will vary.

Page 32
Answers will vary but should follow a logical order.

Page 33
1. a vent on the side of the volcano;

Page 33 (continued)
2. a large herbivorous dinosaur; 3. gently pushed to get his attention; 4. the same through the whole; 5. branches, chewed; 6. many, late; 7. short instrumental passage, repeating; 8. smallest building blocks of matter, positively charged particles in an atom, negatively charged particles in an atom, particles with no charge in an atom

Page 34
1. D.; 2. B.; 3. G.; 4. F.; 5. E.; 6. K.; 7. I.; 8. H.; 9. A.; 10. C.; 11. J.; Answers will vary.

Page 35
1. B.; 2. C.; 3. B.; 4. A.; 5. A.

Page 36
1. Don't look a gift horse in the mouth.; 2. A penny saved is a penny earned.; 3. A miss is as good as a mile.; 4. Don't make a mountain out of a molehill.; 5. A fool and his money are soon parted.; Extra: Hitch your wagon to a star.

Page 37
1. C.; 2. B.; 3. C.; 4. A.; 5. B.; 6. B.; 7. C.; 8. B.; 9. A.; 10. A.

Page 38
1. the side of a road in a milkweed patch; 2. Audrey, Jade; 3. Audrey needs four more caterpillars for school.; 4.–5. Answers will vary.

Page 39
1. at the Field Museum in Chicago, in the past; 2. on a trail in a wagon on the way to California, in the past; 3. in her bedroom in Idaho, in the future; 4. in the woods in Oregon, in the present; 5. in history class, in the future

Page 40
1. present, Answers will vary.; 2. past, Answers will vary.; 3. present, Answers will vary.; 4. future, Answers will vary.; 5. past, Answers will vary.

Page 41
1. Porchia has to clean her room, but the movie will start soon.; 2. Tony is skating in a dangerous

Answer Key

Page 41 (continued)

way.; 3. Darryl wants to try out for the play, but he doesn't have a ride home.; 4. Ana cannot wear her sweater because the button came off.; 5. Eric does not have enough money to buy an MP3 player.

Page 43

1. C.; 2. D.; 3. B.; 4. A.; 5. B.

Page 45!

1. bones losing mass and becoming more likely to break or fracture; 2. collapsed vertebrae, incredible back pain, spinal deformities; 3. because kids do not get enough calcium and if they do not grow enough bone, it cannot be rebuilt; 4. by the age of 18; 5. It has calcium.; 6. can eat other dairy products or green vegetables; 7. It leaches calcium from the bones.; 8. exercise, eat a balanced diet, do not smoke; 9. Answers will vary.

Page 47

1. C.; 2. A.; 3. C.; 4. C.; 5. A.; 6. B.; 7. Answers will vary.

Page 49

E, F, H, I, D, A, G, J, C, B; 1. solid, liquid, gas; 2. Answers will vary but may include: rivers, glaciers, and oceans.; 3. snow, rain; 4. Answers will vary but may include: drinking, bathing, cooking, and growing plants.; 5. salt; 6. heat, wind, and increased surface area

Page 50

7. B.; 8. C.; 9. B.; 10. A.; 11. B.; 12. B.; 13. B.; 14. C.; 15. B.; A. water as a gas; B. Water vapor rises and cools, Condensing on particles, like dust. Millions of these drops form clouds.

Page 51

1. D., E., J.; 2. C., F., H.; 3. B., I., L.; 4. A., G., K.

Page 52

topic—infectious disease; main idea—Viral infectious diseases are contagious.; major detail—epidemic; minor details—Answers will vary but may include: affects a large number

Page 52 (continued)

of people, infection spreads outside a limited group of people, can last for a long time, plague.; major detail—pandemic; minor details—answers will vary but may include: more widespread than an epidemic, established around the world, spread of smallpox among Native Americans.; major detail—endemic; minor details—Answers will vary but may include: present in certain areas of the population all of the time; often caused by an abnormality in plant or animal life, malaria.

Page 53

Topic: Machines need energy to work.; Main Idea: Energy comes from many sources.; 1. fossil fuels; A. come from earth; B. fuel power plants, automobiles, other machines; 2. wind; A. powers windmills; B. is converted into electricity, pushes gears, or pumps water; 3. water; A. dams used to converted energy into electricity, B. possibility of using ocean waves and tides; 4. solar energy; A. solar cells change sunlight into electricity; B. power cars and electrical devices and heat homes

Page 55

main idea—vertebrates are animals that do not have backbones. major details—Order will vary but should include: amphibians, birds, fish, mammals, reptiles.; minor supporting details: Answers will vary. Accept any reasonable answer.

Page 56

1. A., 2; 2. B., 3; 3. B., 5; 4. B., 6; 5. A., 2; 6. B., 5; 7. B., 6 and 8; 8. A., 8; 9. B., 7

Page 58

A. reoccurring; B. interconnecting passageways that let oxygen and carbon dioxide pass between the body and the outside air; C. the bronchi squeeze too tightly, and the brachial tree produces too much mucus, which traps carbon dioxide; D. what causes airway to

Page 58 (continued)

constrict and produce more mucus; E. allergens, irritants, virus, bacteria, exercise, stress

Page 60

1. glaciers that were in the area moved, gouged the land, and filled the lakes with water; 2. drinking water, power plants and manufacturing, recreation, transportation, fishing;
Lake Erie—9,910;
Lake Huron—23,000
Lake Michigan—22,300
Lake Ontario—7,320
Lake Superior—31,700

Page 61

1. inside Jeffrey and Julia's house; 2. the flyswatter hitting the surface; 3. Jeffrey left the sliding door open.; 4. She knows how they fly.; 5. Jeffrey, because it is between Julia's dialogue; 6. Answers will vary.

Page 62

1. Y; 2. N; 3. N; 4. N; 5. N; 6. Y; 7. N

Page 63

1. early morning; 2. waiting for the bus; 3. A; 4. other kids waiting for the bus; 5. they thought a car was the bus; 6. school bus, school, the road, backpack

Page 65

1. have mass, take up space; 2. From left to right and top to bottom: solid, gas, liquid, solid, gas, liquid; 3. Answers will vary.; 4. Two objects cannot occupy the same space at the same time.; 5. Answers will vary but may include: solid, has shape, is black and white; 6. put it in water, cut it in half; 7. Yes, I have mass and take up space.; 8. mixture

Page 67

1. beetles, bugs, buggers, insects, crawlies, critters; 2. light-colored paint, cracks around the windows and air conditioner; 3. vacuum them, caulk cracks around windows and vents; 4. They eat harmful insects, providing less need for pesticide.; 5. when they take over, and if you try

Summer Bridge Reading RB-904096

Answer Key

Page 67 (continued)

to move them, they secrete liquid; 6. She liked them until they got in the house. Ian says that his mom usually likes them, but now, she's going "bonkers."; 7. It helps them retain heat when they live in cooler climates; 8. sides of house, upstairs ceiling, behind the curtain, in the bathroom, the screens

Page 68

1. 2; 2. 3; 3. 1; 4. 3; 5. 2; 6. 2; 7. 2; 8. 3; 9. 2; 10. 3; 11. 1; 12. 2; 13. 2; 14. 3; 15. 3; 16. 3; 17. 1; 18. 1; B. 3, because there is more information to talk about; C. Level 1: Do, Will; Level 2: Where, What, When; Level 3: How, Why

Page 69

1. excited and happy; 2. irritated and crabby; 3. frogs began croaking, ducks began quacking, the wind was blowing, waves came on shore; 4. Answers will vary.

Page 70

1. Main Idea: household measuring tools; Nonsupportive Detail: Carpets help keep your feet warm.; 2. Main Idea: rain forest plants; Nonsupportive Detail: Rain forests have animals, like monkeys and sloths.; 3. Main Idea: Computers have many uses; Nonsupportive Detail: Computers even come in many different colors.; 4. Main Idea: superstitions; Nonsupportive Detail: Many people think that superstitions are silly.; 5. Main Idea: People react differently to anesthesia.; Nonsupportive Detail: Anesthesia makes surgery easy for people because they don't experience any pain.; 6. Main Idea: Limiting television viewing time is important.; Nonsupportive Detail: Watching educational television is better than watching horror shows.

Page 71

1. B.; 2. A.; 3. C.; 4. B.

Page 72

1. pull upper lashes over lower, press a cool, wet washcloth on it, flush eyes with warm water, go to

Page 72 (continued)

the emergency room; 2. A.

Page 74

Answers will vary.

Page 75

1. an extinguished fire; 2. Blaze extinguished—the sun going below the horizon; Smoldering—the shades of pink, red, purple, and orange expanding above the horizon; Blanket of ash—the sky graying at dusk; Speckled with fireflies—the stars sparkling across the sky; 3. Answers will vary.

Page 77

1. B.; 2. D.; 3. C.; 4. A.; 5. B.; 6. D.; 7. C.; 8. A.

Page 79

1. alliteration; 2. onomatopoeia; 3. metaphor; 4. rhyme; 5. assonance; 6. same; 7. meter; 8. rhythm; 9. like; 10. personification; 11. simile

Page 80

1. someone getting out of bed; 2.–3. Answers will vary.

Page 81

1. A.; 2. B.; 3. B.; 4. A.; 5. B.; 6. B.; 7. B.; 8. B.; 9. B.; 10. C.

Page 82

collection of maps and images, gives definitions and pronunciations of words, collection of articles about different subjects, collection of specialized terms, list of topics and page numbers in a book, collection of synonyms of words; 1. dictionary; 2. thesaurus; 3. atlas; 4. dictionary; 5. glossary; 6. index; 7. encyclopedia; 8. glossary; 9. atlas; 10. encyclopedia

Page 83

1. B.; 2. A.; 3. C.; 4. C.; 5. C.; 6. A.; 7. B.; 8. B.

Page 84

1. appendix; 2. table of contents; 3. index; 4. bibliography; 5. acknowledgements; 6. copyright page

Page 85

Specific Details: The brain allows you to access vivid mental images,

Page 85 (continued)

emotions, and even smells when you hear about, read about, or think about certain events.; Each person sees a mental picture based on his own experience.; . . . all of your past knowledge impacts what you comprehend.; Each time a tie, or reference, is made between bits of mental information, it provides additional routes for retrieving it again from the billions of thoughts that have been placed into your mental haystacks.; Places: Your past knowledge can come from personal experience, things you have seen in electronic format, books, or information someone else has shared with you.

Page 86

1. Text: He finds a berry patch and picks some berries to eat., Meg: Every summer, we pick strawberries, raspberries, and blueberries.; Text: He gets a stomachache., Meg: getting a stomachache from eating too many berries on an empty stomach is also a familiar feeling. 2. B.; 3. Both books are about boys who must find shelter and survive in the wilderness. 4. Answers will vary.

Page 88

1. Iesha; 2. Iesha; 3. Jackie; 4. Jackie; 5. both; 6. Jackie; 7. both; 8. Iesha; Answers will vary.

Page 90

1. 1950; 2. one year; 3. 1890; 4. Harriet Tubman; 5. 1878; 6. 1882; 7. House of Representatives; 8. Frederick Augustus Douglass; 9. no, did not earn degree until 1837; 10. Lewis Latimer

Page 91

1. Answers will vary.; 2. B.; 3. C.; 4. A.;

Page 92

1. 9:30 P.M.; 2. the amount of sleep owed to the body; 3. it allows the body to rest and repair itself; 4. irritable, cannot concentrate, emotional, slow reactions; 5. REM sleep

Page 93

Answers will vary.